IMAGES
of America

The Jewish Community of Atlanta

On the Cover: Enrico Leide. The son of an Italian rabbi, Enrico Leide immigrated to the United States and became a noted concert cellist, music instructor, and orchestra conductor. From 1920 to 1930, Leide served as the founding conductor of a nascent group of musicians who adopted the name Atlanta Symphony Orchestra. While unrelated to the Atlanta Symphony Orchestra of today, the organization provided an early framework for arts institutions in the city. Leide later conducted the New York Philharmonic Orchestra and the American Symphony Orchestra. Pictured with the early Atlanta Symphony Orchestra at Stone Mountain Park around 1923, Leide is seated front and center wearing a fedora and overcoat. (Courtesy of the William Breman Jewish Heritage Museum.)

IMAGES
of America

THE JEWISH COMMUNITY OF ATLANTA

Jeremy Katz
Foreword by Dr. Eric L. Goldstein

ISBN 978-1-4671-0585-9

Published by Arcadia Publishing
Charleston, South Carolina

Printed in the United States of America

Library of Congress Control Number: 2020940746

For all general information, please contact Arcadia Publishing:
Telephone 843-853-2070
Fax 843-853-0044
E-mail sales@arcadiapublishing.com
For customer service and orders:
Toll-Free 1-888-313-2665

Visit us on the Internet at www.arcadiapublishing.com

DEDICATION. To Gabrielle, the light of my life, for your endless love and support. (Author's collection.)

Contents

Foreword

When I arrived at Emory as an undergraduate student in 1988, my interest in Jewish history led me to seek out everything I could find in the university's library about Atlanta's Jewish past. I was not disappointed. I discovered that gifted scholars, including Mark Bauman, Arnold Shankman, and Steven Hertzberg, had written pioneering studies of Atlanta Jewry and that local historians Janice Rothschild Blumberg, Doris Goldstein, and Sol Beton had chronicled the life of several Jewish congregations. There was also an effort by the Jewish Federation of Greater Atlanta to begin gathering original records of the Jewish community.

In 2000, after my graduate training in Jewish history at the University of Michigan, I was fortunate to be able to return to Emory as a professor of American Jewish history. Arriving back in Atlanta, I was astounded to find how much more work had been done during my absence on the history of the city's Jews. The most important reason for this heightened interest was the 1996 founding of the William Breman Jewish Heritage Museum and its Ida Pearle and Joseph Cuba Archives for Southern Jewish History. What had earlier been a small collection of records stored in a back room at the Jewish Federation of Greater Atlanta was now a full-fledged regional Jewish museum with its own facility and a growing archive widely consulted by scholars and researchers.

Not only did I begin to visit the Breman regularly to advance my own interests, I also sent my students there to find original material for their research papers. I was honored in 2006 when the founding executive director of the Breman, Jane Leavey, and the founding archivist of the Cuba Archives, Sandra Berman, suggested me as the author of *A History of Jews in Atlanta: To Life*, published to mark the centennial of the Jewish Federation of Greater Atlanta. This project led to an even deeper appreciation on my part for the Breman's amazing collections and devoted staff.

Now, 14 years later, Jeremy Katz, the current archivist of the Cuba Archives, has compiled a beautiful book that not only brings the history of Atlanta Jewry up to date, but also presents a rich array of previously unpublished photographs and historical insights that have emerged from the expanding collections he oversees. *The Jewish Community of Atlanta* is a testament to the continued growth and dynamism of Atlanta Jewry, which continues to make history every day, as well as to the ongoing commitment of the Breman to tell the stories of this vibrant community in new and accessible ways.

—Dr. Eric L. Goldstein
Judith London Evans Director, Tam Institute for Jewish Studies
Emory University

Acknowledgments

When I moved to Atlanta in 2013 to start working at the William Breman Jewish Heritage Museum, I knew only a handful of people in the city. I was taking a leap of faith inspired by my parents, Drs. Allan and Linda Katz, who always encouraged me to follow my interests and passions. Even while I pursued a bachelor of arts degree in history at The Ohio State University with no definitive career in sight, they wholeheartedly supported my curiosities and endeavors. None of us expected then that an interest in history would lead to intimately working with one of the most unique archival collections in the country.

I have deep gratitude and admiration for my esteemed mentors and colleagues at Wright State University, the American Jewish Archives, and the Breman. Your expertise and passion for the field of public history is an inspiration that continues to inform all my career decisions. I am also beholden to my life partner, Gabrielle Adler, who provides unconditional love and encouraging support for my career.

This book would not have been possible without support from both staff and board members of the Breman. Special thanks go to executive director Leslie Gordon, board chair Lori Shapiro, board member Miles Alexander, and legal counsel James Trigg.

I am forever indebted to the review committee that painstakingly pored through the text and images. These members include Elaine Alexander, Sandra Berman, Judy Cohen, Marilyn Ginsberg Eckstein, Doris Goldstein, Evan Kananack, Aaron Levi, Dr. Catherine Lewis, Lindsay Resnick, Carla Silver, and Jeannette Zukor. The book would not be what it is today without your invaluable edits and feedback.

The author's royalties from the sale of this book are supporting the operations of the Breman. By purchasing this book, you are directly contributing to the preservation and interpretation of Southern Jewish history and Holocaust education.

Please note that this book is not a comprehensive history of the Jewish community of Atlanta. It merely scratches the surface of the story and photograph collections at the Breman, which number tens of thousands of images. Despite the limitations, I hope the pages that follow will help shed more light on the all-too-often overlooked story of Jewish life in Atlanta and the American South.

Unless otherwise noted, all images are courtesy of the Ida Pearle and Joseph Cuba Archives for Southern Jewish History at the William Breman Jewish Heritage Museum.

INTRODUCTION

We expect much of Atlanta. The city has been fearfully devastated during the late war. . . . Still, it is a center of commerce, and the reasons which caused it to be built are yet active enough to be the means of its restoration. Israelites will, to a certainty, take their share in the regeneration of Georgia.

—Rabbi Isaac Leeser, 1867

Atlanta is a city based on compromise, convenient geography, and human engineering. Surveyors chose the first piece of flat land south of the Appalachian Mountains as zero mile for three major railroads: the Western & Atlantic, the Macon & Western, and the Georgia Railroad. The fortuitous decision to develop this tract of frontier land created one of the most important railroad junctures in the Southeast, which effectively connected every major city in Georgia to the rest of the country.

Originally called Terminus, then Thrasherville, Marthasville, and finally Atlanta (the female iteration of "Atlantic" in the Western & Atlantic Railroad), the city was incorporated in 1847. Two years prior, Jewish businessmen Henry Levi and Jacob Haas moved their general store six miles west from Decatur, Georgia, to the burgeoning city. On the eve of the Civil War, the Jewish population of Atlanta reached 50. Although they accounted for only one percent of the total population, Jews disproportionately represented ten percent of the city's business owners.

The Civil War demonstrated the strategic importance of the upstart city. Less than 20 years old, Atlanta had become the industrial heart of the Confederacy. The Battle of Atlanta destroyed almost half the city, much of which was in the manufacturing hubs downtown. Atlanta's burning represented a turning point in the war and initiated Union general William T. Sherman's March to the Sea, the death knell for the Confederacy. Jews served on both sides of the conflict. A book published in 1895 by Simon Wolf estimated that more than 8,000 Jews served in the Civil War, including several Medal of Honor recipients, with more than 150 Jews serving in Confederate regiments throughout Georgia.

Reconstruction brought tremendous economic opportunity. Atlanta quickly rose from the ashes as the capital of the "New South." Jews flocked to Atlanta in pursuit of the American dream. With unique connections to Northern markets, much-needed resources, and capital, Jews brought tremendous prosperity to the city. In the South, social dividing lines were drawn by color of skin rather than religion, and as a minority population, Jews were widely accepted in both the Black and White communities. With the ability to navigate between diverse groups, Jews thrived in politics and business as well as in religious and social life.

Favorable conditions in the flourishing city, coupled with deteriorating conditions in Europe, attracted diverse Jewish communities to Atlanta. German-speaking Jews from Central Europe were the first major group to settle in the city, soon followed by Yiddish-speaking Eastern European Jews and Ladino-speaking Sephardic Jews. Social dividing lines based on intra-ethnic biases soon formed as each community established its own congregations and social clubs. Only the tragedy of the Holocaust and the birth of the State of Israel in the mid–20th century inspired the Jewish community to focus on shared values rather than perceived differences.

Despite its general acceptance, the Jewish community of Atlanta was not immune to discrimination and bigotry. In fact, two of the most infamous cases of antisemitism in America occurred in Atlanta. The lynching of Leo M. Frank and the bombing of the Temple made international headlines and traumatized members of the Jewish community. These blatant acts of hatred remind us that even though antisemitism and xenophobia may ebb and flow during times of prosperity, they often violently erupt during times of rapid change and uncertainty. In every instance of adversity, the Jewish community banded together to support each other and overcome challenges.

Similar to the boom following the Civil War, the civil rights movement and the 1996 Summer Olympics reshaped the city. Atlanta's Jewish community expanded beyond the city limits and grew into one of the country's largest Jewish population centers. Simultaneously, a proliferation of innovative organizations cropped up catering to every aspect of Jewish life.

Since its inception, the Jewish tenet of *tzedakah* (charity) has shaped the community's history. From establishing the first nonprofit in the state of Georgia to creating free health clinics that provide services to those in need, the Jewish community of Atlanta has supported itself and cared for the overall welfare of the general public.

Atlanta's Jewish community is a microcosm of Jewish life in America. Its stories weave together similar narratives told throughout the country—peddlers becoming established businessmen and creating enterprises of all sizes, assimilation into local cultures, intra-ethnic biases within the Jewish community, significant acts of charity, and periodic instances of brutal and violent antisemitism. Overarching themes in American Jewish history take on a fascinating character when viewed as part of Atlanta's unique story.

Atlanta has evolved from a frontier railroad town to a thriving international city. This book chronicles the remarkable resilience and achievements of the Jewish community and the contributions it has made to the "Gate City of the South" from its creation to the present day.

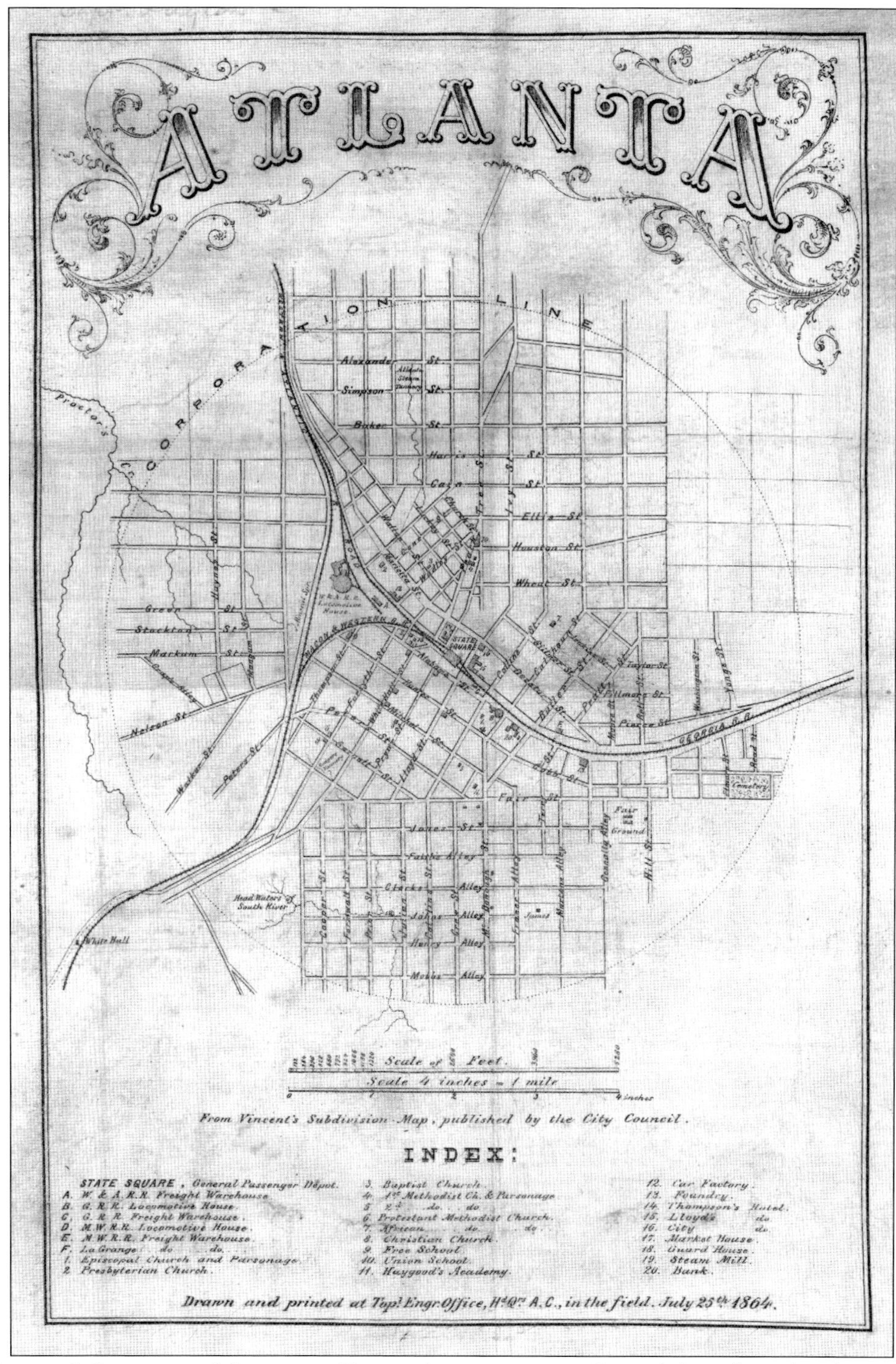

VINCENT'S SUBDIVISION MAP OF THE CITY OF ATLANTA, 1864. Created three days after the Battle of Atlanta during the Civil War, this map illustrates the three railroads that united here. Known as zero mile, this convergence provided a steady stream of raw goods, materials, and entrepreneurial trailblazers that fueled the city's growth. (Courtesy of the Library of Congress.)

One

The Gate City

We congratulate ourselves because nothing is so indicative of a city's prosperity as to see an influx of Jews who come with the intention of living with you.

—*Atlanta Daily Herald*, May 25, 1875

The Civil War left Atlanta decimated, but determined to rebuild. Pioneer Jews who settled in Atlanta during Reconstruction experienced a hospitable city that welcomed them with open arms. Although Black Americans were newly emancipated, social lines were indelibly divided by color of skin rather than religion. Members of the Jewish community enjoyed first-class citizenship, perhaps for the first time in their lives, allowing them to play a vital role in Atlanta's resurgence and reinvention, helping the city earn the moniker Gate City of the South. As a thriving gateway between the North and South, Atlanta was fertile ground for achieving the American dream.

Most Jews who settled in Atlanta soon after the Civil War claimed Central European ancestry and had already lived in the United States for several years. Somewhat assimilated into American culture and with connections to Northern markets, they thrived in commercial, fraternal, philanthropic, political, religious, and social life. During this time, the Jewish community formed its first religious congregation, Aaron Haas became mayor pro tempore and helped found the Piedmont Driving Club, David Mayer helped establish the Atlanta Public Schools system, Jacob Elsas assisted in creating the Georgia School of Technology (today the Georgia Institute of Technology), Jacobs' Pharmacy served the first glass of Coca-Cola as a fountain drink, Rich's department store welcomed its first customers, the national fraternal organization B'nai B'rith formed a local chapter, and Victor Kriegshaber initiated a campaign that brought to Atlanta what became Emory University. Simultaneously, the first nonprofit in Georgia—the Hebrew Orphans' Home—was founded, providing a much-needed safety net for the Jewish community's most vulnerable children throughout the Southeast.

During these pivotal years, Jewish pioneers laid the foundation that the Jewish community and many other Atlanta residents continue to enhance and rely upon today.

CAROLINE A. HAAS. Jacob Haas, one of the first Jews to settle in Atlanta, had a daughter, Caroline, the first Jewish person born in Atlanta. The land that became Atlanta was once Cherokee and Creek Native American territory. The initial settlements surrounded forts that were built during the War of 1812. The Georgia gold rush in 1829 brought more newcomers to the region, who began to displace the Native American populations. Reflecting the system of segregation and the ideology of racial hierarchy that shaped Southern culture, White Atlantans often celebrated Caroline Haas as the "first White girl" born in the city, as did the publisher of the early-1900s postcard below memorializing her birthplace. (Below, courtesy of Special Collections and Archives, Georgia State University Library.)

Hebrew Benevolent Society. In 1860, Atlanta's developing Jewish community founded the Hebrew Benevolent Society, which purchased a section of burial plots in the city-owned Oakland Cemetery. Following Jewish law, the section was walled off from the rest of the cemetery. At the time, it was also the section of the cemetery closest to Jerusalem. Today it is known as the Old Jewish Burial Grounds and is one of three Jewish sections at Oakland Cemetery.

First Jewish Wedding. Rabbi Isaac Leeser of Philadelphia visited Atlanta in early 1867 to officiate the first Jewish wedding in the city. He recognized the potential of Atlanta's growing Jewish community and encouraged them to form a congregation. Following his advice, the community established the Hebrew Benevolent Congregation on April 1, 1867. The Temple, as it came to be known, has since played a pivotal role in Atlanta's Jewish life and is one of the city's largest congregations today. Pictured here are Emilie Baer and Abraham Rosenfeld on their wedding day, January 1, 1867.

HEBREW BENEVOLENT CONGREGATION (THE TEMPLE). On August 31, 1877, the Hebrew Benevolent Congregation dedicated the first synagogue built in Atlanta. The *Atlanta Constitution* reported, "The dedication of the Jewish Temple yesterday was one of the most impressive scenes that ever occurred in Atlanta." The towering Moorish-style stone-and-brick building had keyhole windows and minaret-like spires topped with onion domes. It was on the corner of Forsyth and Garnett Streets and served the congregation until 1902, when a new synagogue was erected on the corner of Pryor and Richardson Streets. The congregation quickly outgrew that building as well and moved to its current location on Peachtree Street in 1931.

Rich's Dry Goods Store. In 1867, Hungarian Jewish immigrant Morris Rich arrived in Atlanta and opened M. Rich & Co. This small dry goods store quickly grew into the largest department store chain in the Southeast through exceptional customer service and cutting-edge marketing techniques. Rich's visionary leadership, commitment to its customers, and civic duty inextricably linked the store to Atlanta's commercial, political, social, cultural, and architectural development. When Atlanta could not afford to pay public employees during the Great Depression, the store cashed promissory notes in hard currency, allowing teachers and municipal workers to pay for rent, food, and other necessities. In 1936, Morris Rich's son Walter Rich presided over the first Atlanta Dogwood Festival, an annual event the city still cherishes. In 1948, the philanthropic Rich Foundation gifted a radio station to the Atlanta and Fulton County school systems that continues to operate today as 90.1 WABE, Atlanta's NPR station. Although Rich's was purchased by Federated Department Stores in 1976 and became Macy's in 2005, the legacy continues through the Rich Foundation, which supports numerous worthy causes in the Atlanta area.

Hirsch's. Founded in 1863 by German Jewish immigrant brothers Henry, Joseph, and Morris Hirsch, Hirsch's was an Atlanta menswear retailer for more than 100 years. The Hirsch brothers played leading roles in both the Jewish and general communities and helped establish the Temple, the Hebrew Orphans' Home, the Morris Hirsch Clinic, Henry Grady Memorial Hospital, and Hirsch Hall Nursing Home. Pictured is the 100th anniversary celebration of the store in 1963.

Regenstein's. Julius Regenstein, a German Jewish immigrant, founded Regenstein's in 1872. It became one of the most popular women's apparel stores in the South. The family-owned store was eventually sold in 1976. Still standing today, the Art Deco building was constructed in 1929 at the corner of Peachtree Street and Andrew Young International Boulevard.

FULTON BAG AND COTTON MILL. Born in Germany, Jacob Elsas immigrated to the United States at the age of 18 with one dollar in his pocket. A keen businessman, Elsas noticed cotton harvested in the South was then shipped to Northern cities to be milled. Recognizing an opportunity to industrialize the South, he incorporated the Fulton Bag and Cotton Mill in 1889, which manufactured cloth and paper containers. By the turn of the 20th century, the company was Atlanta's largest employer. To accommodate the workforce, a mill town sprang up around the factory, which is visible at bottom right below. This vibrant neighborhood is known today as Cabbagetown. To develop skilled engineers for maintaining the factory, Elsas helped found what is now the Georgia Institute of Technology. His son Oscar Elsas became one of the first students enrolled at the new school—he later succeeded his father in running the business. Pictured above is the senior management of the mill, including Jacob and Oscar Elsas seated front and center wearing black suits and ties.

David Mayer. David Mayer settled in Atlanta prior to the Civil War. During the war, he worked with Georgia governor Joseph E. Brown as his commissary officer and became an important leader in Atlanta's reconstruction. Mayer assisted the Hebrew Benevolent Society in acquiring the first Jewish burial section at the city-owned Oakland Cemetery. Most notably, he helped lead the effort to establish the Atlanta Public Schools. As vice president of the board of education for many years, he advocated allowing excused absences for Jewish children observing religious holidays.

Aaron Haas. One of the first Jews to settle in Atlanta, Haas was elected to Atlanta's city council in 1874. The following year, he became mayor pro tempore. Haas was a founding member of the Piedmont Driving Club, a private social club that was later closed to Jews. He also cofounded the Haas-Howell Company, one of Atlanta's oldest insurance companies. It now operates as a commercial real estate firm known as Haas and Dodd.

JACOBS' PHARMACY. Joseph Jacobs was born in America to German Jewish immigrant parents and raised in Jefferson, Georgia. Upon completing his formal education at the University of Georgia and the Philadelphia College of Pharmacy, Jacobs opened Jacobs' Pharmacy Company in downtown Atlanta. Soon after, another Atlanta pharmacist, Dr. John S. Pemberton, approached Jacobs to sell his newly created tonic, Coca-Cola, in the soda fountain at Jacobs' Pharmacy. The first glass of Coca-Cola was sold on May 8, 1886. Jacobs owned a one-third share of Coca-Cola company stock, but after falling on hard times, he sold his shares to Asa Candler for $2,000. Despite this shortsighted business decision, Jacobs went on to establish a successful career. By the time of his death in 1929, he owned eight pharmacies around Atlanta. His son Sinclair Jacobs took over the business and grew the chain to 21 pharmacies throughout the South, eventually selling to Revco Drugs following World War II. Pictured at right is Joseph Jacobs in 1928. Below is Jacobs' Pharmacy in downtown Atlanta in 1917.

Hebrew Orphans' Home. Established in 1889 by B'nai B'rith, the Hebrew Orphans' Home was the first nonprofit in the state of Georgia. The Venetian-style building was in the heart of the Jewish community on Washington Street between Love and Little Streets. The central building, clinic, dairy, servants' cottage, and playground occupied an entire square block. Between 1889 and 1930, the facility cared for hundreds of Jewish children from all over the Southeast. During the interwar years, it helped resettle Jewish refugee children fleeing deteriorating conditions in Europe. In 1948, the organization was renamed Jewish Children's Service Inc., and provided foster home placements and adoptions. In 1988, the organization adapted to the needs of the community and transitioned into the Jewish Educational Loan Fund, which has since provided interest-free educational loans to Jewish students throughout the Southeast. (Courtesy of the Kenan Research Center at the Atlanta History Center.)

Proto-Jewish Community Center. Due to its central location and plethora of amenities, the Hebrew Orphans' Home essentially served as a Jewish community center. The grounds boasted a skating rink, basketball court, tennis court, playground, and baseball diamond. The residents were encouraged to participate in community activities and develop valuable social skills. The remedial classes offered by the home helped the children gain employable skills to quickly find jobs upon graduating. Pictured above and below are images of the grounds.

STAFF AND RESIDENTS. Ralph A. Sonn served as superintendent of the Hebrew Orphans' Home from 1889 until his retirement in 1924. Under his direction, children received religious instruction at local synagogues, attended classes at nearby Fraser Street School, and were trained as typists, stenographers, plumbers, and printers. Pictured above are residents of the Hebrew Orphans' Home standing on the steps to the orphanage with Superintendent Sonn and his wife, Dora, around 1910.

VICTOR HUGO KRIEGSHABER. The child of German Jewish immigrants, Victor Kriegshaber became a successful businessman in Atlanta. He served as a charter member of the Rotary Club, president of the chamber of commerce, and president of the Hebrew Orphans' Home. Under his guidance, the chamber of commerce launched a campaign to bring to Atlanta what is now Emory University. Located in the Little Five Points neighborhood, his Victorian-style home was listed in the National Register of Historic Places in 1979.

Joseph Hirsch. German Jewish immigrant Joseph Hirsch became a manufacturer, banker, volunteer fireman, city council member, alderman, and a founder of the Hebrew Orphans' Home. In 1890, while serving as a city council member, he championed the creation of Henry Grady Memorial Hospital, which became one of the largest public health care systems in the world. Upon his death in 1914, Hirsch bequeathed funds from his estate to establish a home for the aged at Grady Hospital. Hirsch Hall Nursing Home, as it became known, contained living accommodations, classrooms, a library, and laboratories for the hospital's nursing school.

Albert Steiner. German Jewish immigrant Albert Steiner became president of the Atlantic Brewing Company in 1897. One of the brewery's longest-produced beers, Steinerbru, was named after him. Upon his death in 1919, Steiner bequeathed funds from his estate to establish a clinic that researched the causes of cancer and provided treatment to indigent cancer victims. The Steiner Clinic, as it became known, is a part of Henry Grady Memorial Hospital.

Two

THE MELTING POT OF DIXIE

Decatur Street is the home of humanity as it is. . . . Here bearded mountaineers from Rabun County brush shoulders with laborers fresh from the Old Country. Jewish shopkeepers pass the time o' day with the clerk of the Greek ice cream parlor next door. The Yankee spieler cries his wares and the Confederate veteran buys 'em . . . types of the south which could be seen in no other city in the land in all their native picturesqueness. Decatur is the melting pot of Dixie.

—*Atlanta Journal Magazine*, May 18, 1913

In 1888, Henry Grady, a journalist and publisher of the large and influential *Atlanta Constitution*, coined the term "New South" in a speech to the New England Society of New York. If the Old South represented nostalgia for genteel agrarianism dependent on slavery, the New South championed diversity and industrialization predicated on highly educated, skilled workers. According to Grady, Atlanta was the capital city of the New South, leading the region in scientific innovation and industrial growth.

Now fully recovered from the Civil War, Atlanta's strategic railroad connections allowed easy access to both Northern and Southern goods. Industry in the city flourished by the turn of the 20th century. Economic opportunities, combined with the ideals of the New South, attracted recently arrived immigrants to Atlanta. A diverse population mushroomed as thousands flocked to the city in search of employment and a better quality of life. Simultaneously, turmoil in Eastern Europe and the collapse of the Ottoman Empire led to an influx of Jewish refugees seeking asylum in America. The increasingly prosperous city of Atlanta proved to be fertile ground for Jewish refugees.

Although originally founded as an Orthodox synagogue in 1867, the Hebrew Benevolent Congregation (the Temple) eventually adopted the liturgy and customs of Classical Reform Judaism. Not comfortable with this style of worship, newly arrived immigrants began establishing their own congregations. The Eastern European community founded Ahavath Achim Synagogue in 1887, Congregation Shearith Israel in 1904, and Anshi S'fard in 1913. The Sephardic community organized Congregation Or VeShalom in 1914. Today, these congregations form the rich variety of religious and cultural expression in Atlanta.

The escalation in immigration to Atlanta and a swelling of urban population also ushered in a rise of antisemitism and xenophobia. The social clubs that Jews helped found now denied them membership as the city became increasingly insular.

PEDDLERS. Many Jewish immigrants in the late 19th and early 20th centuries eventually found their way to Atlanta after peddling goods throughout the countryside. Upon accumulating enough capital, itinerant peddlers sought hospitable towns to build retail establishments that soon formed the backbone of many local economies throughout the region. Pictured around 1910 is Teddy Blumenthal with his horse and cart in north Georgia, peddling his goods.

H. MENDEL & COMPANY. Founded in 1890 by Eastern European immigrant and one-time peddler Hyman Mendel, H. Mendel & Company grew into the largest dry goods supplier in Atlanta. Mendel provided goods on credit to peddlers and often helped them open retail establishments in the city and elsewhere. The business was family-run until 1973.

Cotton States Exposition. In 1895, Atlanta hosted the Cotton States and International Exposition, which attracted nearly 800,000 visitors. The exposition was Atlanta's opportunity to demonstrate to the rest of the country and world that it was a progressive, industrial city. Held in present-day Piedmont Park, the exposition featured 13 main buildings and 6,000 exhibits focused on key Southern industries such as agriculture, mining, manufacturing, and railroads. Emanuel Rich, brother of the founder of M. Rich Dry Goods, chaired the event and is pictured in the middle of the three men standing together facing the camera.

H. Silverman Company. Owned by Harry Silverman, this cigar store was so popular that the corner of Peachtree and Broad Streets became known as "Silverman's Corner." One of the store's most successful marketing ploys was the "Silverman's Baby Lions" sales promotion. Silverman at first sought to buy live lion cubs, but at a prohibitive price of $500 per cub, he decided instead to rent them for $20 a week.

Rabbi David Marx. David Marx arrived in Atlanta in 1896 to serve as the Temple's first American-born rabbi—a position he held for the next 50 years. Born in New Orleans and trained in Classical Reform Judaism, Rabbi Marx quickly changed many of the congregation's traditional religious practices in an attempt to achieve greater assimilation into the general community. By the turn of the 20th century, Marx had eliminated the bar mitzvah ceremony, removed head coverings and prayer shawls from the sanctuary, and inaugurated Sunday services. Along with many Reform rabbis of the era, he held staunch anti-Zionist views, arguing that Jews were a religious community rather than a peoplehood or nation.

Ahavath Achim Synagogue. Founded in 1887 by a small number of Eastern European Jews, Ahavath Achim built its first synagogue on the corner of Gilmer Street and Piedmont Avenue in 1901, pictured here. The congregation remained there until 1920, when a new synagogue was constructed on Washington Street, which was also quickly outgrown. In 1956, the congregation moved to its current location on Peachtree Battle Avenue. Opposed to the Classical Reform customs observed by Central European Jews at the Temple, Ahavath Achim practiced Orthodox Judaism until 1952, when it joined the Conservative movement.

AHAVATH ACHIM SECTION AT OAKLAND CEMETERY. In 1892, the Temple acquired additional land at city-owned Oakland Cemetery and sold one-quarter of it to Ahavath Achim Synagogue. The tight grouping of plots and modest traditional Orthodox-style monuments in this section vary considerably from the more spacious and elaborate aboveground mausoleums in the Temple section. The forest-like plots represent a growing community with less wealth and a smaller degree of assimilation than their coreligionists.

JEWISH EDUCATIONAL ALLIANCE (JEA). Founded in 1909, the JEA served as the central hub for Atlanta's Jewish community. In its early years, it facilitated the acculturation of newly arrived immigrants by offering English lessons, instruction for citizenship, and lectures on American history. In 1946, the JEA changed its name to the Atlanta Jewish Community Center and later relocated to a larger space on Peachtree Street. Today, it is the Marcus Jewish Community Center of Atlanta and is located on a sprawling suburban campus at Zaban Park in Dunwoody. This c. 1930 photograph shows the JEA building on Capitol Avenue.

Diverse Clubs. Offering meeting spaces for a diverse range of clubs, the Jewish Educational Alliance served as the home base for many organizations that celebrated Jewish culture and heritage. Pictured on March 18, 1917, is the Yiddish Progressive Dramatic Club, which operated out of the JEA.

Meyer Balser. Meyer Balser grew up around the corner from the Jewish Educational Alliance building and was one of its most active members. When the JEA became the Atlanta Jewish Community Center in 1946, Balser was elected as its first president. Throughout his 10-year tenure, he helped raise funds to create a larger facility on Peachtree Street. Pictured here is Balser in his JEA basketball team uniform in 1925.

National Council of Jewish Women (NCJW). Since its founding in 1895, the Atlanta Section of the NCJW has been committed to community service by addressing issues related to women, children, and education. The organization helped found the Free Kindergarten Association, the Jewish Educational Alliance, and the Children's Dental Clinic. During the World Wars, it helped displaced persons resettle. Today, the organization provides assistance to the Jewish and general communities locally, nationally, and internationally. Pictured here are officers of the NCJW Atlanta section around 1910.

First Sephardic Wedding. As the Ottoman Empire declined, antisemitism in the region increased, prompting a wave of Jewish immigration to America. The wedding of Ezra and Julia Tourial in January 1912 signaled a growing contingent of Sephardic Jews in Atlanta. Two years later, these families established Congregation Or VeShalom, where Sephardic customs and traditions continue to be important hallmarks of this religious community today.

SHOE STORES. A popular occupation in the growing Sephardic community was the shoemaking trade. By 1914, sixty-seven percent of the employed Sephardic Jews in Atlanta were shoemakers, most of whom owned their own shops. The Moreland Avenue Shoe Store was owned by Solomon Levy, who can be seen operating a machine near the front of the store around 1910.

RABBI JOSEPH I. COHEN. Born in Istanbul, Rabbi Cohen served in the Turkish army during World War I and later worked for the British government in Jerusalem. After returning to Turkey to train as a rabbi, he accepted his first pulpit in Cuba. In 1934, Rabbi Cohen moved to Atlanta where he served as spiritual leader of Congregation Or VeShalom for 35 years.

Michael Greenblatt. The first bandmaster at Georgia Tech, Michael Greenblatt is credited with writing and arranging the school's fight song, "Ramblin' Wreck." During the Spanish-American War, he served as a trombonist in a military band. Greenblatt later held the title of bandmaster for the Atlanta police, Shriners, Elks, Georgia Power Company, and the Georgia Guard Band. He is thought to have originated the "derby hat technique" to muffle the sound of a trombone. This c. 1910 photograph shows Greenblatt leading the Georgia Tech band.

Morris Hirsch Clinic. After helping found both Hirsch's clothing store and the Temple, Morris Hirsch generously established a free health clinic in 1911. The Morris Hirsch Clinic, as it became known, provided outpatient medical services to the city's most vulnerable. In 1956, the clinic was renamed and repurposed as the Ben Massell Dental Clinic, which continues to operate today, providing free dental care to those in need. Pictured around 1915 is an unidentified man standing at the entrance to the clinic.

Federation. In 1905, the Atlanta Jewish community joined the federation movement and established the Federation of Jewish Charities. The central fund provided free English language classes, interest-free loans, and case workers for family counseling to quickly Americanize newly arrived Jewish immigrants. Today, the organization is known as the Jewish Federation of Greater Atlanta and continues to offer vital services that address current social and economic issues confronting the community. Pictured here is Harry Koval advertising the Atlanta Federation for Jewish Social Service in 1937.

Rhoda Kaufman. Born in Columbus, Georgia, Rhoda Kaufman moved to Atlanta after graduating from Vanderbilt University. She quickly became active in progressive social initiatives, working for the Associated Charities of Atlanta, Georgia Board of Public Welfare, Atlanta Family Welfare Society, and the Social Planning Council of Atlanta. In 1930, she accepted Pres. Herbert Hoover's invitation to participate in the Conference of Social Work, which examined social welfare conditions in the United States. Pictured around 1910 are Rhoda Kaufman (left) and her sister Bernice.

Annie Teitelbaum Wise. Born in Hungary, Annie T. Wise immigrated to America, settling in Atlanta at a young age. She attended Atlanta public schools, later becoming a school educator and administrator. In 1914, Wise became principal of Commercial High School. Under her guidance, enrollment grew to 1,500. In 1917, at the age of 51, she enrolled in Georgia Tech's Evening School of Commerce and became the first woman to graduate from the school in 1919. Pictured around 1914 is Wise, second from left, with fellow staff members of Commercial High School.

Hadassah. Founded in 1916, the Atlanta chapter of Hadassah is committed to educating, engaging, and empowering its members and the community. While membership in the National Council of Jewish Women was mostly comprised of German Jews, Hadassah members were predominantly Eastern European Jews. The Atlanta chapter of Hadassah recently celebrated its 100th anniversary and boasts more than 3,500 members. Pictured here is a Hadassah sewing group around 1930.

Standard Club. Established in 1867 as the Concordia Club, the Standard Club is the oldest Jewish social club in Atlanta. Throughout its early history it maintained a closed membership policy, open primarily to well-established German Jews. This policy, in part, led to the establishment of additional social organizations like the Jewish Progressive and Mayfair Clubs, which met the needs of other growing segments of Atlanta's Jewish community. Pictured is a Spanish dress ball at the Standard Club in 1925.

Osceola Club. Excluded from the German Jewish clubs, Eastern European Jews formed a myriad of short-lived social groups including the Don't Worry Club, Harmonie Social Club, and the Osceola Club, pictured here. The most successful of the Russian immigrant organizations was the Jewish Progressive Club (JPC), founded in 1913.

Jewish Progressive Club. Unable to join the Standard Club due to intra-ethnic biases and high membership fees, Eastern European Jews established the Jewish Progressive Club. Both clubs held similar social functions and provided a gathering space for their respective communities. Pictured here is the JPC hiking club on December 14, 1924.

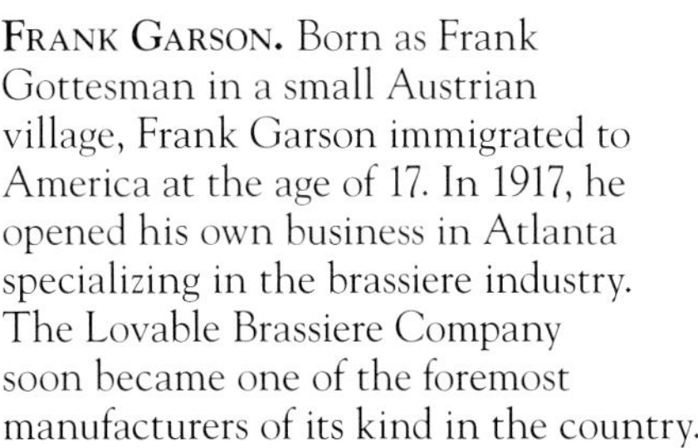

Frank Garson. Born as Frank Gottesman in a small Austrian village, Frank Garson immigrated to America at the age of 17. In 1917, he opened his own business in Atlanta specializing in the brassiere industry. The Lovable Brassiere Company soon became one of the foremost manufacturers of its kind in the country.

One Man Boom. In 1888, the same year that Henry Grady delivered his famous New South speech, Ben Massell, as a child, emigrated with his family from Kovno, Lithuania, and settled in Atlanta. He later became one of the most influential members of the Jewish community. In 1918, he established Massell Properties, and by 1953, the commercial real estate company had built more than a thousand buildings in Atlanta. Mayor William Hartsfield called Ben Massell a "One Man Boom." Pictured above is Mayor Hartsfield cutting the ribbon to a new building with Massell standing front and center around 1950. Below is Massell with Eleanor Roosevelt when she visited Atlanta for an Israel Bonds dinner in 1962.

Jake Abel. Born in Russia, Jacob Abelson pioneered the sport of boxing in the early 20th century as a well-known welterweight fighter under the name "Jake Abel." During World War I, he served in the US Army and was crowned champion of the Allied Expeditionary Forces boxing tournament. The prince of Wales, later crowned King George V, proclaimed him his favorite boxer. After the war, Abelson married Charnye Bressler, a longtime Atlanta resident active in Ahavath Achim Synagogue's Sisterhood and the Atlanta chapter of Hadassah. Together, they ran the Jefferson Hotel in downtown Atlanta. Pictured is Jake Abel (left) in the boxing ring around 1920.

Alfred Garber. Alfred Garber and his sisters Frieda Garber Goldstein Karp and Janet Garber Nadel became residents of the Hebrew Orphans' Home after their father died and their mother was diagnosed with tuberculosis. Alfred was one of the first residents to receive an interest-free loan from the home to attend the University of Georgia, where he earned an accounting degree. In 1940, he started Young & Garber, which grew into one of the largest accounting firms in the region. Pictured is Alfred with his sister Janet around 1924.

Grocery Stores. Many early immigrants from Eastern Europe found it economically viable and profitable to establish small grocery stores in blue-collar and Black neighborhoods. Having undergone discrimination themselves, Jewish grocery store owners sympathized with the plight of Black Americans and welcomed them into their stores, often extending credit during difficult times. A recent immigrant, Max Feldman sent this picture of his grocery store to his wife, Eva, who had remained in Russia with their two sons. Within five years, Feldman had the resources to

send for the rest of his family. Numbered items are as follows: 1. icebox, 2. scale, 3. cash register, 4. glass candy display case, 5. dry goods display case, 6. flour storage area fenced to keep out rats, 7. boxes of produce and nuts, 8. Feldman's favorite kitchen stove and pan he used for personal cooking, 9. canned food, and 10. eggs. The door at left led to the storage room, which doubled as Feldman's bedroom.

ACCULTURATION. Second-generation Eastern European Jews quickly assimilated into American society. Exemplifying this was Harry Kuniansky, the son of Lewis Kuniansky, a Russian immigrant who opened a grocery store in Atlanta. Harry is pictured playing football for the University of Georgia Bulldogs around 1940.

HAROLD HIRSCH. Harold Hirsch was born in Atlanta in 1881 to German Jewish immigrants. He served as both general counsel and vice president of The Coca-Cola Company, helping to develop and patent the iconic logo and uniquely shaped bottles. In 1932, the University of Georgia School of Law named its new building in his honor—Harold Hirsch Hall. In 1936, Hirsch spearheaded the creation of the Atlanta Jewish Welfare Fund to address the mounting needs and struggles of Jews in Nazi Germany. The Welfare Fund is now the Jewish Federation of Greater Atlanta.

Rabbi Tobias Geffen. Tobias Geffen was born in Kovno, Lithuania, on August 1, 1870. Educated at a yeshiva in Slobodka, he immigrated to the United States in 1903. After serving as rabbi at congregations in New York City and Canton, Ohio, he accepted the pulpit at Congregation Shearith Israel in Atlanta—where he remained for the next 60 years. Rabbi Geffen is best known for his efforts to certify Coca-Cola as kosher. He received a list of ingredients, a closely guarded trade secret, on the condition he not disclose them. After persuading Coca-Cola executives to replace animal fat–based glycerin with vegetable-based glycerin, the rabbi issued a responsum in 1935 declaring the drink kosher. He also certified a kosher-for-Passover version of the cola, which substitutes cane sugar for corn syrup. Rabbi Geffen is seen here celebrating Passover with his grandson David in 1950.

ORKIN PEST CONTROL. At the age of 14, Otto Orkin started his pest control company by selling rat poison door-to-door. In 1926, he moved the company from Pennsylvania to Atlanta and began advertising with the now-familiar red and white diamond logo. Before selling to Rollins Inc. in 1964, Orkin grew into one of the largest pest control companies in the country. The company is still based in Atlanta today. Pictured here is an Orkin Pest Control horse and cart around 1930.

MAX CUBA. A juggernaut in communal leadership, Max Cuba served in numerous community leadership roles. His civic activities included being elected to the city council and being selected as the inaugural chairman of the Atlanta–Fulton County Joint Board of Planning and Zoning. In the Jewish community, Cuba served as president of Ahavath Achim Synagogue, the Jewish Progressive Club, and the Israel Bond Organization. His accounting firm, Max Cuba & Company, audited Jewish-owned businesses and organizations including Orkin Pest Control and the Federation.

Three

A Powder Keg

The South is barely half educated. Whatever there is explicable in the murder of Leo M. Frank is thus explainable. The South is a region of illiteracy, blatant self-righteousness, cruelty and violence. Until it is improved by the infusion of better blood and better ideas it will remain a reproach and a danger to the American Republic.

—*Chicago Tribune*, August 18, 1915

Early in the 20th century, rapid growth of industry and the increasingly diverse population of the city's inhabitants tested the limits of the New South ideals. Disaffected White people who were struggling with the economic and cultural effects of industrialization and urbanization often fell back on racist assumptions while trying to make sense of their rapidly changing world. This tinderbox led to an upsurge in lynching and other forms of anti-Black violence, such as the Atlanta Race Riot of 1906, in which dozens of Black citizens were killed and mutilated by mobs of angry White men. The aftermath left Atlanta further segregated and socially stratified.

Much less typical than attacks on Black people, but also a product of the social turmoil that accompanied Atlanta's rise as an industrial city, were accusations that Jews were responsible for the excesses of the capitalist culture that was reshaping the South. The most dramatic example of this occurred in 1913 when news of a 13-year-old factory worker named Mary Phagan, found murdered in the basement of the National Pencil Company in the heart of downtown Atlanta, ignited like a powder keg throughout the city. Leo M. Frank, a Northern Jewish industrialist and superintendent of the factory, was the last person to admit to seeing Phagan alive. He was subsequently arrested and charged for the crime. After a trial rife with antisemitic undertones, Frank was convicted of murder and sentenced to death by hanging.

Georgia governor John Slaton recognized the injustice of the trial proceedings and commuted Frank's sentence to life in prison. Enraged by this decision, a cabal of prominent individuals calling themselves the "Knights of Mary Phagan" abducted Frank from prison and lynched him near Phagan's home in Marietta.

The tragic murder of Phagan and unjust lynching of Frank resulted in widespread trauma throughout the Jewish community. The trial boosted support for the formation of the Anti-Defamation League, which became a well-respected Jewish organization that continues today, combatting antisemitism and all forms of hatred. The lynching also motivated the resurrection and resurgence of the Knights of the Ku Klux Klan, a hate group that continues to vilify and attack Black and Jewish communities in America.

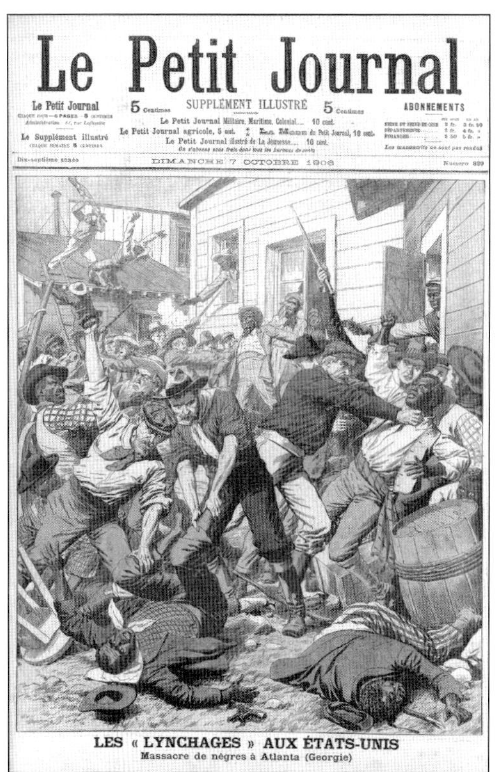
Le Petit Journal

Le Petit Journal

Le Supplément illustré

5 Centimes SUPPLÉMENT ILLUSTRÉ 5 Centimes

Le Petit Journal Militaire, Maritime, Colonial.... 10 cent.

Le Petit Journal agricole, 5 cent.

Le Petit Journal illustré de La Jeunesse.... 10 cent.

ABONNEMENTS

Les manuscrits ne sont pas rendus

Dix-septième année

DIMANCHE 7 OCTOBRE 1906

Numéro 829

LES « LYNCHAGES » AUX ÉTATS-UNIS

Massacre de nègres à Atlanta (Georgie)

ATLANTA RACE RIOT. In September 1906, a race riot engulfed the city. The riot started with unsubstantiated claims in local newspapers of Black men drinking in Jewish-owned saloons on Decatur Street and subsequently sexually assaulting White women. Rioters murdered more than two dozen Black citizens and wreaked havoc on businesses and property. This flashpoint highlighted the simmering social and racial tensions in Atlanta at the turn of the 20th century. International press reported the story, and the negative publicity damaged Atlanta's reputation as a tolerant and progressive city. Pictured is a French newspaper reporting on the riot.

SALOONS. Leading up to the 1906 race riot, Jewish-owned saloons faced antisemitic attacks by the media and teetotaling populists for serving members of the Black community. Russian Jewish immigrant Mike Shurman owned four such saloons in Atlanta, some in the Decatur Street district, one of which is pictured here around 1900.

Greenblatt Bros. Pawn Shop. Greenblatt Bros. supplied guns to Fulton County sheriff John W. Nelms in 1906 to help control the Atlanta Race Riot. Founded by their father, Benjamin Greenblatt, the company was owned by brothers Morris (left) and Sam Greenblatt (right).

Ivy League Educated. Leo M. Frank received a bachelor of science degree in mechanical engineering from Cornell University in 1906. Following graduation, he traveled to Germany to study pencil manufacturing at Eberhard-Faber. In 1908, he moved to Atlanta to accept the job of superintendent at the National Pencil Company, where his uncle Moses Frank was a large shareholder. Pictured here is Leo M. Frank (far left) in his dormitory room around 1905.

Mary Phagan. Born in Alabama but raised in Atlanta, Mary Phagan's father died a few months before her birth. Her widowed mother returned to the family's ancestral home near Marietta in Cobb County, 20 miles northwest of Atlanta. In 1912, Phagan started working at the National Pencil Company. She is pictured here shortly before her death in 1913. (Courtesy of the Adolph Ochs Papers, New York Public Library.)

Love and Marriage. Leo M. Frank met Lucille Selig soon after moving to Atlanta in 1908, and the two married on November 30, 1910. Although new to the South, Frank was readily accepted and formed important social connections in the Atlanta Jewish community. In 1912, he was elected president of the Gate City Lodge of B'nai B'rith, the largest and oldest Jewish fraternal organization in Atlanta. Pictured are Frank and Selig at Grant Park on July 17, 1909.

Lucille Selig Frank. Leo M. Frank's wife, Lucille Selig, was born on February 19, 1888, to Josephine and Emil Selig. Her great-grandfather Levi Cohen was a founding member of the oldest Jewish synagogue in Atlanta, the Hebrew Benevolent Congregation, more commonly known as the Temple. Shortly after her husband's lynching, Lucille moved to Nashville for a few years but soon returned to Atlanta. She never remarried. Her cremated remains are buried between her parents' graves in the Jewish Hill section of Oakland Cemetery.

Emil Selig. Lucille Selig's father, Emil, worked for West Disinfecting, which proclaimed itself the largest manufacturer of disinfectants in the world. Emil's brother, Simon Selig, started Selig Chemical Company in 1896, which grew into a premier Atlanta business. The family sold the business to another Jewish-owned chemical company, Zep, in 1968. Pictured in 1904 is West Disinfecting manager Emil Selig (second from right).

Sigmund Montag. German Jewish immigrant Sigmund Montag was the majority shareholder of the National Pencil Company. In 1906, he established Montag Brothers Inc., which later became one of the leaders in the stationery industry. Their Blue Horse trademark, imprinted on tablets and notebook paper, became a household name. Montag also started one of the first rebate reward programs. Especially popular with schoolchildren, customers were encouraged to clip and mail in the Blue Horse logo in exchange for prizes.

Atlanta Police Station. The Atlanta Police Department conducted a botched investigation into Mary Phagan's tragic murder. Investigators trampled over the crime scene, destroying footprints and fingerprints, and misplacing hard evidence. The resulting trial boiled down to unsubstantiated oral testimony. Several key witnesses were questioned at the police station until they repeated the prosecutor's version of events.

STATE OF GEORGIA V. LEO M. FRANK. The trial occurred during the heat of summer, so the courtroom windows were opened to increase ventilation. This open-air environment subjected the courtroom to the influence of the rowdy crowds gathered outside during the two-month trial. Fearing mob justice and "lynch law" if Frank were acquitted of the crime, he was notably not present in the courtroom when his verdict was read. At the end of the trial, the jury found Frank guilty and sentenced him to death by hanging. Pictured is lead prosecutor Hugh Dorsey questioning the National Pencil Company's night watchman Newt Lee on the first day of the trial, July 28, 1913. (Courtesy of Special Collections and Archives, Georgia State University Library.)

JIM CONLEY. The main witness against Leo M. Frank was the sweeper at the National Pencil Company. The prosecution team relied heavily on his testimony to buttress their argument that Frank killed Mary Phagan. During the appeals process, Conley's own lawyer, William Smith, professed his belief that Conley was solely guilty of the crime. Many historians today believe Conley was Phagan's true murderer due to inconsistencies in his testimony and the deposition of Alonzo Mann in 1982. (Courtesy of the Adolph Ochs Papers, New York Public Library.)

FIDDLIN' JOHN CARSON. During the case, Cobb County native John Carson wrote a song titled "The Ballad of Mary Phagan," slandering Leo M. Frank as Mary Phagan's killer. He later recorded what are widely accepted as the first country music songs. Carson worked at the Fulton Bag and Cotton Mill and was a participant in the employee labor strike that occurred during the case. Pictured here is Carson being evicted from company housing during the strike in 1914. (Courtesy of Special Collections and Archives, Georgia State University Library.)

HENRY A. ALEXANDER SR. A native Atlantan, Henry Alexander Sr. was the grandson of Aaron Alexander, one of the first Jews of American birth to settle in Atlanta. In 1914, Alexander joined the appeals team representing Leo M. Frank. His analysis of the murder notes found at the crime scene played an important part in the appeals process. Alexander was active in both the general and Jewish communities and was a founder of the Atlanta Historical Society, known today as the Atlanta History Center. He also filed the articles of incorporation for the Atlanta Art Association, today the High Museum of Art.

Hugh Dorsey. Despite being close college friends, Hugh Dorsey and Henry Alexander Sr. found themselves on opposing sides during the Leo M. Frank case. Dorsey served as the lead prosecutor, and Alexander was an appeals attorney. Their differences caused an irreconcilable rift in their relationship. Dorsey later served as governor of Georgia, elected in part due to his successful prosecution of Frank. Pictured around 1894 is Dorsey (left) with Alexander while classmates at the University of Georgia.

Appeals. Leo M. Frank appealed his conviction, a process lasting two years and ultimately reaching the US Supreme Court, where the guilty verdict was upheld seven-to-two. The two dissenting justices argued that Frank failed to receive a fair trial due to the influence of the unruly crowd outside the courtroom. These arguments established precedent that is now common law. Pictured is Frank in the Fulton County Prison in 1914.

Gov. John M. Slaton. One of the most popular governors of his day, Governor Slaton was positioned for a senatorial career after his governorship. After Leo M. Frank's final unsuccessful appeal to the Supreme Court, Slaton reviewed all available trial evidence and records and decided to commute Frank's sentence from death by hanging to life in prison on June 21, 1915. In response to the commutation, a mob gathered outside the governor's mansion, forcing Slaton to call in the National Guard for his own protection.

State Prison Farm. The night before Governor Slaton publicly announced the commutation, state officials, under the cover of night, surreptitiously shepherded Leo M. Frank from the Fulton County Prison in downtown Atlanta to the state prison farm in Milledgeville, Georgia, to serve out his life sentence. On the night of August 17, 1915, a group of conspirators abducted Frank from the state prison farm without firing a shot, drove him to Marietta, and lynched him early the next morning just outside of town.

Lynching. The epidemic of lynching throughout the South was often met with public fanfare. Soon after the lynching of Leo M. Frank, crowds gathered by the thousands to view his body (pictured). Mob violence broke out, and people mutilated his corpse and took souvenir pieces from the scene. Such actions were common after the lynchings of more than 450 Black people in Georgia between 1882 and 1930.

The Lynch Mob. The lynching was carefully orchestrated by influential members of the greater Atlanta community, including Joseph M. Brown, former governor of Georgia; Eugene Herbert Clay, former mayor of Marietta; and E.P. Dobbs, who was mayor of Marietta at the time. Like many other lynchings at the time, all participants escaped justice for the crime. Pictured on August 18, 1915, is the crowd that gathered in Marietta Square following the lynching.

TOM WATSON. A leading demagogue and populist of the time, Thomas E. Watson consistently used his newspaper, the *Jeffersonian*, for diatribes aimed at stoking his readers' resentment against Leo M. Frank. His vitriolic paper incited mob violence, leading to the lynching of Frank following the commutation of his sentence. Shortly thereafter, Watson advocated for the Ku Klux Klan to regroup. He later served as a US senator from Georgia. A statue in his honor stood atop the steps to the Georgia State Capitol until 2013.

GRAVESITE OF LEO M. FRANK. On August 20, 1915, Frank was interred at Mount Carmel Cemetery in Brooklyn, New York. The bottom of his headstone reads "Semper Idem"—"Always the Same" in Latin. Even though countless Jews immigrated to America to escape persecution, Atlanta and American Jewry now faced the same violence, born from antisemitism, they had encountered in their home countries. Following Frank's lynching, the Jewish community receded from public life. More than a decade passed before a member of the community ran for public office again in Atlanta.

AFTERMATH. The murder of Mary Phagan and lynching of Leo M. Frank had lasting repercussions that continue to be felt today. The trial boosted support for the newly formed Anti-Defamation League, which tirelessly combats all forms of hatred throughout the United States and around the world. Frank's lynching also motivated the resurrection and transformation of the Ku Klux Klan, a modern, active, and virulent hate group. Pictured is a postcard memorializing the reorganization of the Ku Klux Klan atop Stone Mountain on November 25, 1915.

ALONZO MANN. In 1982, Alonzo Mann, a 14-year-old office boy at the National Pencil Company in 1915, confessed to seeing Jim Conley carrying Mary Phagan's body to the basement of the factory. His deposition encouraged new efforts to issue a posthumous pardon to Leo M. Frank that the state ultimately denied. Subsequent efforts by the Anti-Defamation League and activists in the Atlanta Jewish community prompted the Georgia State Pardons and Parole Board to issue a partial pardon in 1986. Without addressing guilt or innocence, the state recognized its failure to protect Frank and bring his killers to justice. Pictured is 85-year-old Alonzo Mann paying his respects at the grave of Mary Phagan on March 7, 1983. (Photograph by Nancy Rhoda; courtesy of *USA Today*.)

Ku Klux Klan Activity. A century after the murder of Mary Phagan and the lynching of Leo M. Frank, Atlanta still grapples with its aftermath. Protesting immigration to Marietta, Mary Phagan's home, this rally on April 20, 2013, took place at the steps of the Georgia State Capitol in the shadow of Tom Watson's statue. The recent resurgence in demagoguery, populism, racial divisions, and yellow journalism eerily mirrors events in the city more than 100 years ago.

Historical Marker. Originally erected in 2008, this historical marker commemorates the lynching of Leo M. Frank. Due to construction projects, it was removed in 2014 by the Georgia Department of Transportation. On August 23, 2018, the marker was rededicated alongside a monument memorializing lynching victims across the country and state of Georgia. Pictured are, from left to right, Patricia Meagher, Georgia Historical Society; Jerry Klinger, Jewish American Society for Historic Preservation; Shelley Rose, Anti-Defamation League Southeast; and Rabbi Steven Lebow, Temple Kol Emeth. (Courtesy of the Anti-Defamation League.)

Four

A Diverse Community Uniting

During my early teens, which started about 1930, the division between North Side and South Side, German Jews and Russian Jews, was clear, accepted, and respected.

—David Macarov, unpublished autobiography

The 1996 Broadway play *The Last Night of Ballyhoo* is perhaps the best-known depiction of the divisions amid and diversity within the Jewish community of Atlanta between the World Wars. Written by native Atlantan Alfred Uhry, the drama chronicles Sunny Freitag, a young woman of German Jewish descent who falls in love with Joe Farkas, a young Jewish man of Eastern European descent who works in her uncle's factory. Sunny's relationship with Joe forces her and her family to confront long-standing intra-ethnic biases.

German Jews who settled in Atlanta in the mid-19th century had already assimilated, amassed wealth, and raised their social status a generation before the Eastern European Jews who arrived later in the century. Besides economic and social elements, other divisive issues between immigrant groups included religious practices and Zionism, the movement to reestablish a Jewish homeland in Palestine. The tragedy of the Holocaust and support for the birth of the State of Israel prompted Atlanta's diverse Jewish community to begin focusing on its shared values instead of its differences.

The rise of patriotism within the United States during World War II also helped unify the community. Jewish Atlantans from all backgrounds contributed to the war effort on both the front lines and the home front. After the war, patriotic efforts involved helping in the resettlement of Holocaust survivors. In 1948, the Jewish community rallied around the formation of the State of Israel, raising millions of dollars to support the burgeoning country. Years later, after the fall of the Iron Curtain, Atlanta Jews galvanized support for the resettlement of Soviet Jews who came to the community in large numbers.

These poignant events highlighted the community's shared values and collective heritage. Despite different customs, languages, religiosity, wealth, or social status, Atlanta's Jews found common ground in the mid-20th century, leading to a stronger and more cohesive community.

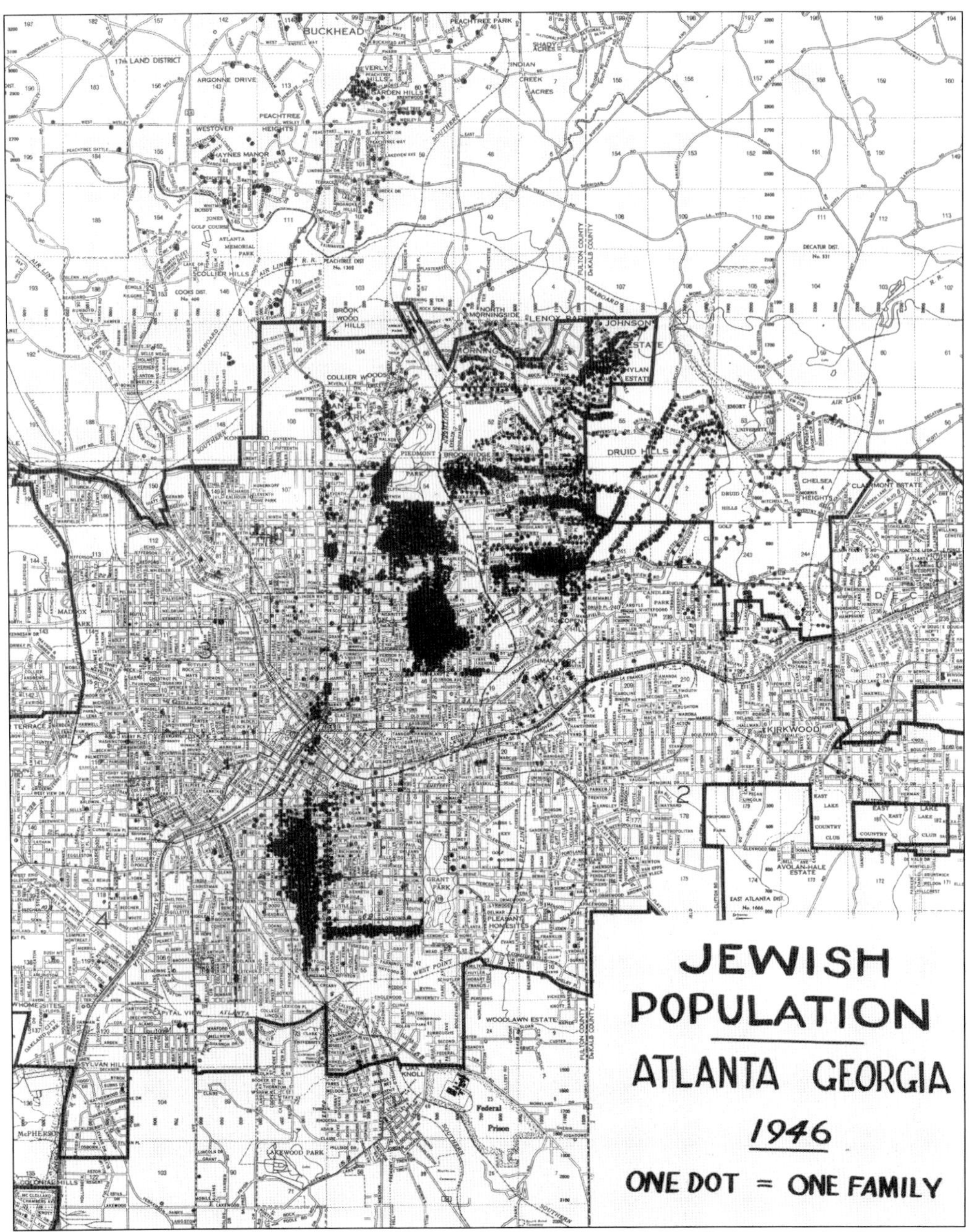

Division. Created by the National Jewish Welfare Board for the Jewish Community Council of Atlanta, known today as the Jewish Federation of Greater Atlanta, this map clearly shows the social and residential divisions of Atlanta's Jewish population. The mass on the south side of town mainly consisted of Sephardic and Eastern European Jews living in modest urban dwellings. On the north side were primarily German Jews with elevated social status living in newly established suburbs. Their separate houses of worship and social clubs were located in their respective neighborhoods. The dividing line was Ponce De Leon Avenue, a major thoroughfare in Atlanta.

Ballyhoo. Starting in 1931, Ballyhoo was a social occasion that became an annual tradition through the 1950s. Held at the Standard Club, the dance provided an opportunity for Jewish youth of German descent from around the Southeast to fraternize. Ballyhoo was the backdrop for Alfred Uhry's Broadway play *The Last Night of Ballyhoo*. Pictured is a group on the way to Ballyhoo in 1950.

Mayfair Club. The Mayfair Club welcomed members of the Jewish community curious to explore common ground between the German and Eastern European Jews. In 1938, the club opened a building on Spring Street and was active until it was destroyed by a fire in 1964. These members were on their way to the first dance of the Mayfair Club on December 16, 1930.

Rabbi Harry H. Epstein. Born in Lithuania, Harry Epstein immigrated to the United States with his family in 1909 and settled in Chicago. In 1928, after studying at rabbinical schools in Chicago, New York, Lithuania, and Palestine, Rabbi Epstein became the spiritual leader of Ahavath Achim Synagogue in Atlanta. He held the position for the next 54 years. During his tenure, he became involved with many local and national organizations and was a staunch supporter of Zionism. He also enacted the progressive ritual of bat mitzvah in 1941, the first rabbi in the region to do so.

Joseph Berman. Born in Camilla, Georgia, Joseph Berman became the first member of the Jewish community to run for public office in Atlanta since the lynching of Leo M. Frank. Serving as a city councilman from 1931 to 1935, he played a leading role in implementing significant improvements to Candler Field, today's Hartsfield-Jackson International Airport. His efforts helped the airport grow into the world's busiest by the end of the century. Berman (second from left) is pictured at the dedication of a new beacon tower at Candler Field in 1933.

EDWARD M. KAHN. As a child, Kahn emigrated from Bialystok, Poland, to America. He spent his early years in New York City, where he acquired most of his schooling. In 1914, Kahn graduated from the Brooklyn Law School of St. Lawrence University and was admitted soon after to the New York State Bar. In 1920, he moved to Chicago, Illinois, accepting a position as the educational director of the Jewish People's Institute. A strong interest in social work inspired him to take graduate courses in community organization and administration. In January 1928, Kahn accepted the combined positions of executive director for the Atlanta Federation of Jewish Social Service (presently, Jewish Federation of Greater Atlanta), the Morris Hirsch Clinic (Ben Massell Dental Clinic), and the Jewish Educational Alliance (Marcus Jewish Community Center of Atlanta). Later, Kahn also served as executive secretary of the Atlanta Jewish Welfare Fund (established in 1936) and the Atlanta Jewish Community Council (1945), which combined to form the Jewish Federation of Greater Atlanta. He held these various positions until his retirement in 1964. Over the years, Kahn's work helped make the Jewish community more cohesive and unified.

The Temple on Peachtree Street. Under the direction of Rabbi David Marx and designed by the famed Atlanta architectural firm Hentz, Adler, and Shutze, the Temple on Peachtree Street stands as an example of Classical Reform Judaism. Complete with red-white-and-blue stained-glass windows, New England–style pews, and an eternal light strung from a gold Great Seal of the United States, the Temple is a physical representation of assimilation into American society. Constructed in 1931, the building is listed in the National Register of Historic Places and is still used today by the congregation.

Rudolph Adler. A native Atlantan, Adler became one of the city's most prominent architects. After graduating from Columbia School of Architecture, he became a junior partner at the firm Hentz, Reid, and Adler—later Hentz, Adler, and Shutze. The firm became known for its Beaux Arts style and was a founder of the Georgia School of Classicism. Adler is pictured here around 1917 during World War I.

Arbeiter Ring. Founded in 1907 by immigrants from Eastern Europe, the Atlanta chapter of the Arbeiter Ring, known in English as the "Workmen's Circle," promoted Yiddish, education, socialism, culture, and later, Zionism. In 1919, the organization purchased a building on Capitol Avenue where it held meetings and classes. Active throughout much of the 20th century, the Atlanta chapter created a sense of community for this segment of the population. Pictured is the Atlanta chapter of the Arbeiter Ring at Black Rock Park in north Georgia around 1933.

Josephine Joel Heyman. Shortly before the outbreak of World War II, Josephine Joel Heyman taught English to Jewish refugees from Nazi Europe. At the same time, she was an active member of the Association of Southern Women for the Prevention of Lynching. During the 1960s, she became an activist in the civil rights movement. She is pictured here (standing at left) teaching English through the Georgia Farm School and Resettlement Bureau in 1940.

Home Front. Even before the United States formally entered World War II, the Jewish community of Atlanta mobilized in support of the Russian war effort against Nazi Germany. The sewing circle pictured here was organized by the Atlanta chapter of Hadassah around 1941.

Patriotism. The Jewish community of Atlanta was committed to broad patriotic service on all fronts during World War II. In 1945, the secretary of the treasury, Henry Morgenthau, awarded the local chapter of B'nai B'rith Women a certificate of merit for selling more than $1.5 million in war bonds. Pictured is a war bonds fundraising dinner at the Jewish Progressive Club around 1943.

The Ultimate Sacrifice. In 1939, Jack B. Gordon was one of seven Atlantans nominated to attend West Point but failed the medical examination. Undeterred, he was admitted to the first entering class of 90-Day Wonders at the US Naval Academy. Upon graduation in early 1941, he was stationed in the Philippines. Soon after the US entry into World War II, Gordon was taken captive by Japanese forces. He survived the infamous Bataan Death March and endured 31 months as a prisoner of war before perishing on December 15, 1944. He is pictured here in his Reserve Officers' Training Corps uniform at Boys' High School around 1937.

Women's Air Service Pilot. Shortly after graduating from Vanderbilt University, native Atlantan Evelyn Greenblatt Howren began taking flight instruction at Candler Field. She received her pilot's license in 1941 and soon joined the first all-women's squadron of the newly formed Civil Air Patrol. In November 1942, Howren was one of 32 inducted in the first class of Women's Air Service Pilots (WASPs). After the war, she returned to civilian life and became a flight instructor. In 1947, Howren helped organize the Women's Aero Club of Atlanta. Upon retiring in 1983, she continued to fly and kept all required flight qualifications and ratings. In 1994, Howren became the third woman inducted into the Georgia Aviation Hall of Fame. These c. 1943 photographs show her serving with the WASPs during World War II.

PAUL GINSBERG. A Boston native, Paul Ginsberg moved to Atlanta in 1927 to marry Jean Cuba, the sister of Joseph and Max Cuba. He began practicing law in 1930 and held the prestigious roles of Georgia assistant attorney general, assistant solicitor general, and assistant district attorney for Fulton County. One of his most notable accomplishments was the exposure and prosecution of the notorious neo-Nazi group the Columbians. During World War II, Ginsberg distinguished himself on several occasions and received numerous accolades. As the Cold War began, Pres. Harry S. Truman sent Ginsberg on a diplomatic trip around the globe to meet with world leaders to determine if their allegiance leaned toward the East or West. An ardent anti-communist, Ginsberg published a book in 1954 about his experience titled *Wake-Up America*. Pictured above is Ginsberg meeting with President Truman in the Oval Office in 1951. At right, on January 4, 1952, Ginsberg (left) is leaving for his trip around the world to meet with world leaders.

Henry Birnbrey. Henry Birnbrey was born in Dortmund, Germany, in 1923. As conditions for German Jews disintegrated in the 1930s, his parents submitted an application for him to emigrate. Assisted by Jewish Children's Services in Atlanta, Birnbrey was placed in foster care first in Birmingham, Alabama, and then Atlanta. In 1943, he joined the US Army and participated in the invasion of Normandy. After the war, he started a successful accounting firm in Atlanta. Pictured is Birnbrey onboard a ship en route to the United States in 1938.

Cantor Isaac Goodfriend. Born in Poland on January 20, 1924, Cantor Goodfriend survived the Holocaust and settled first in Cleveland, Ohio, and then in Atlanta, where he served as cantor at Ahavath Achim Synagogue for 30 years. In 1977, he sang the national anthem at Pres. Jimmy Carter's inauguration and was appointed by Carter to the President's Commission on the Holocaust in 1979. Pictured is Cantor Goodfriend with the boys' choir at Ahavath Achim Synagogue in 1974.

Benjamin Hirsch. Born just a few months before Hitler came to power, as a young child, Hirsch witnessed the terror of *Kristallnacht* (Crystal Night, or the "Night of Broken Glass"), including the burning of the synagogue his family attended. Recognizing the growing danger, his mother arranged passage for him and four of his siblings on a *Kindertransport*, a rescue mission for Jewish children that relocated them to England. Only nine years old and orphaned by the Holocaust, Hirsch eventually settled in Atlanta, joining his siblings who had arrived before him. He graduated from Hoke Smith High School, then entered the School of Architecture at Georgia Tech. During the Korean War, Hirsch joined the US Army. After the war, he founded the architectural firm Benjamin Hirsch and Associates. His firm designed churches, synagogues, homes, medical emergency centers, and commercial, industrial, and municipal buildings. Picture at right is Hirsch at his bar mitzvah on September 15, 1945. He is pictured below as an architect in 1982.

Memorial to the Six Million. In 1965, Eternal Life–Hemshech, an organization of Holocaust survivors in Atlanta, funded and constructed the second-oldest Holocaust memorial in the country. The building committee consisted of Dr. Leon S. Rosen (chair), Lola Lansky (cochair), Nathan Bromberg (cochair), Abraham Gastfriend, Mala Gastfriend, Gaston Nitka, Rubin Lansky, Rubin Pichulik, Benjamin Hirsch (architect), and Abraham Besser (builder). An annual memorial service is held at the monument on Yom HaShoah, Holocaust Memorial Day, organized by Eternal Life–Hemshech and the William Breman Jewish Heritage Museum. The monument is listed in the National Register of Historic Places.

Congregation Beth Jacob. Founded in 1942, Beth Jacob has grown into Atlanta's largest Orthodox congregation. Located in the Toco Hills neighborhood, the synagogue was designed by Benjamin Hirsch, a congregant of Beth Jacob. Due to the congregation's influence, other Orthodox congregations and day schools have sprouted in the vicinity.

Rubin Pichulik. Born in Poland, Pichulik survived the Holocaust by fleeing to Russia where he and his wife, Sara, spent the war in Siberian slave labor camps. In 1951, the couple settled in Atlanta and eventually opened a grocery store, Jackson Street Market. An early member of Eternal Life–Hemshech, Rubin served on the committee that oversaw the creation of the Memorial to the Six Million at Greenwood Cemetery. He is pictured behind the counter of his grocery store around 1955.

Frances Hamburger Bunzl. Born in Weisbaden, Germany, Bunzl fled to England shortly after the outbreak of World War II and settled in Atlanta in 1941. She served as president of the Atlanta chapter of the National Council of Jewish Women from 1963 to 1967 and as chancellor of the Austrian consulate from 1972 to 1989. In 1988, Bunzl established the timpani chair at the Atlanta Symphony Orchestra in memory of her late husband, Walter H. Bunzl. In 2007, the Frances B. Bunzl Administrative Building at the High Museum was named in her honor. The following year, the Atlanta chapter of the Association of Fundraising Professionals recognized her as Philanthropist of the Year.

STATE OF ISRAEL. The founding of the State of Israel was a momentous occasion for Jews around the world. In 1948, the Atlanta Jewish community celebrated this historic achievement with an outpouring of jubilation and pride at the Jewish Progressive Club (pictured). The tragedy of the Holocaust and birth of the State of Israel helped heal divisions and unify Atlanta's diverse Jewish community.

WILLIAM GAREY. A native Atlantan, William Garey was raised in the Temple's Reform German Jewish community. As a member of the Army Air Force during World War II, Garey traveled to Palestine on days off and felt a strong connection to the growing movement for a Jewish state. When the State of Israel declared independence, Garey answered the call once again and served in the Israeli air force. Pictured around 1948 in Geneva, Switzerland, is Garey (right) with Xiel Federmann, a leading Zionist operative, on a mission to secure supplies for the Israeli air force.

David Macarov. A native Atlantan, David Macarov was raised in the Orthodox Eastern European Jewish community and Congregation Shearith Israel. Soon after serving in the Army Weather Service during World War II, Macarov joined Aliyah Bet, an effort to aid illegal immigration to Palestine during the British Mandate. Macarov moved to Israel in 1947, becoming one of the first Atlantans to make aliyah, the process of acquiring Israeli citizenship. During Israel's War of Independence, Macarov served in the Israeli air force. Pictured is David with his wife, Frieda, and their daughter, Varda, at an Israeli air force camp around 1948.

Golda Meir in Atlanta. Jewish Atlantans have a long history of supporting the State of Israel. Zionist organizations such as the Farband Labor Zionist Order and Zionist Organization of America formed chapters in Atlanta during the early 20th century. The Federation of Jewish Charities, which operated as a centralized fundraising entity of the community, raised significant capital for projects in Israel. Golda Meir (seated at center) is seen here during a visit to Atlanta around 1948.

Joint Trip to Israel. In a show of solidarity, Rabbi Jacob Rothschild (right) and Rabbi Harry Epstein traveled to Israel together, and also cochaired the 1950 Jewish Welfare Campaign. Spearheaded by their spiritual leaders, the divided German and Eastern European Jewish communities started to focus on shared values instead of differences.

The *Southern Israelite*. Originally founded in Augusta, Georgia, in 1925, the monthly publication relocated to Atlanta, where it began circulating statewide and eventually throughout the Southeast. The paper covered news related to Jewish life in the South, national and international issues, the Holocaust, and later, the creation of the State of Israel. Throughout the 20th century, well-respected journalists such as Adolph Rosenberg and Vida Goldgar owned the *Southern Israelite*. The paper operates today as the *Atlanta Jewish Times* with more than 25,000 weekly subscribers.

Henry Sopkin. Classically trained at the American Conservancy of Music, Henry Sopkin founded the Atlanta Youth Symphony Orchestra in 1945. By 1947, the organization had grown into the Atlanta Symphony Orchestra (ASO), which continues to make Atlanta a center for arts and culture regionally, nationally, and internationally. Sopkin served as conductor until 1966 and was instrumental in growing the ASO to a well-respected professional level. The planned giving campaign of the organization is named the Henry Sopkin Circle in his honor.

Harry Robkin. Born in Russia, Harry Robkin became a first section violinist of the Atlanta Symphony Orchestra under the direction of Enrico Leide and later Henry Sopkin. Robkin also served as personnel manager of the symphony, and upon retirement was named personnel manager emeritus. He is pictured here with Frances Wallace (at the piano) and Estelle Karp in 1953, and also on the cover at back left.

JOINT SERVICE. For the first time in the history of the Atlanta Jewish community, the major congregations came together in 1954 for a joint Thanksgiving service. Sponsored by Congregations Ahavath Achim, Beth Jacob, Or VeShalom, Shearith Israel, and the Temple, the service was led by Rabbi Harry Epstein (at the pulpit), Rabbi Emeritus David Marx (far left), Rabbi Tobias Geffen (far right), Rabbi Joseph Cohen (second from right) and Rabbi Emanuel Feldman (third from right). Rabbi Jacob Rothschild (fourth from right) delivered the sermon. Symbolic acts of partnership like this joint service helped create a more close-knit Jewish community.

ATLANTA JEWISH COMMUNITY CENTER. In 1946, the Jewish Educational Alliance changed its name to the Atlanta Jewish Community Center, and in 1956 moved to a new location on Peachtree Street (pictured). The facility included athletic fields, classrooms, and spaces for the community to gather regardless of political, economic, or ethnic differences.

Five

The City Too Busy to Hate

The night was clear and very quiet. A myriad of stars twinkled in the darkened heavens. A city slept—secure and unaware. In a few hours, streets would be busy with cars and sidewalks bustling with fathers, mothers and their children—all hastening to fill countless pews in hundreds of Houses of Worship. For this was the early morning of another Sunday and the city was a city of churches; its citizens a deeply religious folk. But this was destined to be a Sunday morning different from all those that had gone before it. For the date was October 12, 1958—and the city was Atlanta, Georgia.

—Rabbi Jacob Rothschild,
"And None Shall Make Them Afraid" sermon delivered on October 17, 1958

Rabbi Jacob Rothschild moved to Atlanta in 1946 to become the spiritual leader at the Hebrew Benevolent Congregation, commonly referred to as the Temple, the city's oldest Jewish congregation. As a resettled Northerner, witnessing the discrimination and segregation confronting the Black community troubled him. He began preaching support for integration and civil rights. Rabbi Rothschild's outspokenness concerned some members of the Jewish community, especially those who remembered the extreme scrutiny the Jewish community faced after experiencing the tragedy of Leo M. Frank, a Temple member who was lynched in 1915. These fears were realized when the Temple was bombed in the early morning hours of October 12, 1958.

Following the bombing, there was an outpouring of support for the Temple by global political and religious leaders. The baseless act of hatred achieved the opposite effect its perpetrators intended. Instead of scaring the Jewish community into submission, it bolstered the ranks of outspoken supporters for civil rights and bookended the lynching of Leo M. Frank. Once again, the Jewish community felt accepted in Atlanta.

Examining the civil rights movement in Atlanta through a Jewish perspective offers unique insight into the city's history. As a minority group themselves, Jews occupied a rare place between the Black and White communities and held varying views across the sociopolitical spectrum. While some Jewish leaders and businesses advocated for equal rights long before the civil rights movement, others hesitated to upset the status quo. Atlanta's Jewish community played an active role in the civil rights movement and helped to fundamentally change the social fabric of the city.

Prior Tire Company. In 1932, Prior Tire Company became the first private business in Atlanta to hire Black employees for sales positions. Abe Goldstein, who founded Prior Tire in 1920, and his son Leon actively advocated for civil rights through their family-owned business and through their leadership roles in various civic and religious organizations. In the 1990s, Prior Tire reignited the civil rights debate when the business sued the Atlanta Public Schools (APS) system over its affirmative action policy after losing a contract despite submitting the lowest bid. Prior Tire argued that the company had long supported civil rights and that favoring any one group over another was discrimination. APS lost the case and revised its affirmative action policy. Pictured below is the sales and service department of the Prior Tire Company on Peachtree Street in 1941.

LOVABLE BRASSIERE COMPANY. Frank Garson, an immigrant from Austria who became a successful businessman in Atlanta, assembled an integrated workforce as early as the 1930s. When his son Dan took over the business after World War II, he continued the company's progressive hiring practices. Both Frank and Dan Garson were early advocates for civil rights and active members of the Jewish community. Frank Garson (far right) is seen here with employees in 1941.

COLUMBIANS. Founded in Atlanta in the summer of 1946, the Columbians were the first neo-Nazi political organization in the country following World War II. The short-lived hate group terrorized members of the Black and Jewish communities. A decade later, one of their former members, George Bright, was accused of bombing the Temple. Pictured is an undercover investigator holding dynamite confiscated from the Columbians in 1947. (Photograph by Jimmie Fitzpatrick, courtesy of the Associated Press.)

Rabbi Jacob M. Rothschild. Born and raised in Pittsburgh, Pennsylvania, Jacob Rothschild attended rabbinical school in Cincinnati. During World War II, he was stationed at Guadalcanal and became the first Jewish Army chaplain to face combat. Experiencing the ravages of war firsthand, Rothschild became determined to build a better world. In May 1946, he accepted the rabbinate at the Temple, Atlanta's oldest synagogue. He immediately used the pulpit to advocate and preach against segregation, discrimination, racism, and intolerance. The unfortunate result of his outspokenness occurred on October 12, 1958, when the Temple was bombed. The incident shook both its physical and spiritual foundations. In addition to his legacy of social justice that has since become a tenet of the Temple, Rabbi Rothschild also moved the congregation to Traditional Reform Judaism, reintroducing Hebrew to services, reinstating the practice of bar mitzvah, and supporting Zionism.

The Temple Bombing. Just hours after the bomb exploded in the early morning of October 12, 1958, Mayor William B. Hartsfield—who dubbed Atlanta "the City too Busy to Hate"—conducted a live broadcast from the Temple. With the destruction in full view behind him, Mayor Hartsfield declared, "Atlanta has always been a lighthouse of racial and religious tolerance in the South. And we're shocked and amazed that this awful thing could happen in our midst. . . . my friends, here you see the end result of bigotry and intolerance. And whether you like it or not, those who practice rabble rousing and demagoguery are the godfathers of the cross burners and the dynamiters." (Photograph by Dwight Ross Jr., courtesy of the Associated Press.)

Mayor Hartsfield's live broadcast rallied support all over the country for the Jewish community of Atlanta. Hartsfield is seen here inspecting the damage alongside Rabbi Jacob Rothschild. Fortunately, no one was injured or killed by the blast. (Photograph by Dwight Ross Jr., courtesy of the Associated Press.)

Ralph McGill. The day after the bombing of the Temple, Ralph McGill, editor of the *Atlanta Constitution*, published a column titled, "A Church, a School." The scathing rebuke of hatred won McGill the 1959 Pulitzer Prize for editorial writing. Pictured is McGill receiving an award for his "untiring efforts in combating the forces of bigotry" by the Georgia Department of Jewish War Veterans on July 27, 1947.

The Accused Bombers. Although five suspects faced trial for the bombing of the Temple, none were convicted of the crime. The scheme's accused mastermind, George Bright (far left), was tried twice, the first resulting in a hung jury and the second in acquittal. Despite no convictions, the resounding support the Jewish community received following the bombing provided some resolution in lieu of justice. Pictured on October 17, 1958, are the five men accused of the crime at Fulton County Courthouse awaiting their hearing.

Janice Oettinger Rothschild Blumberg. Due to the outpouring of support for the Jewish community following the bombing of the Temple, Janice Rothschild, wife of Rabbi Rothschild, called it the "Bomb that Healed." Janice herself testified against George Bright in both trials. Even though no one was convicted of the crime, the festering wounds from the lynching of Leo M. Frank finally began to heal. Pictured on January 27, 1965, are the Rothschilds with their close friends Coretta Scott King and Rev. Martin Luther King Jr. at the banquet in honor of King receiving the Nobel Peace Prize. (Courtesy of Bill Rothschild.)

Leb's Restaurant. In the summer of 1962, Charlie Lebedin, a member of the Jewish community and owner of Leb's Restaurant, posted a full-page newspaper advertisement welcoming all to celebrate 13 years of business. Civil rights activists attempted to eat at the segregated restaurant but were refused service. Lebedin argued that he would serve Black patrons once other downtown restaurants did. He reluctantly integrated in 1964 after Congress passed the Civil Rights Act. Despite being one of the most popular restaurants in town before the protests, bad publicity from his refusal to integrate ultimately led to its closure. Pictured are protesters outside Leb's in 1962.

Rich's in Downtown Atlanta. One of the largest and most iconic businesses in Atlanta, Rich's became the focus of nonviolent student protests during the civil rights movement. Despite allowing Black customers to try on clothes—albeit in segregated dressing rooms—and offering them credit, unlike many department stores in the South, two of the restaurants in its flagship downtown store were segregated: the Magnolia Tea Room and the Crystal Bridge Café. In October 1960, police arrested Martin Luther King Jr. during a sit-in at Rich's. Some historians argue John F. Kennedy's help releasing King from jail shifted the Black vote from Republican to Democrat and led to his election as president.

MORRIS B. ABRAM. Born in Fitzgerald, Georgia, Abram became a prominent Atlanta lawyer and civil rights activist. In 1954, he campaigned to become the US representative from Georgia's 5th Congressional District (above), which encompasses much of the metro Atlanta area. His progressive platform favoring desegregation cost him the election. Six years later in October 1960, when Rev. Martin Luther King Jr. was arrested for participating in a nonviolent sit-in at Rich's, the Kennedy campaign enlisted Abram's help to negotiate the release of the prominent civil rights leader. In 1963, Abram helped overturn the "county unit system," a Georgia electoral rule that gave disproportionate weight to rural votes over urban votes. He later served as president of Brandeis University, chairman of the United Negro College Fund, president of the American Jewish Committee, and chairman of the National Conference on Soviet Jewry. Pictured below is Abram with Robert F. Kennedy in 1968.

Nobel Peace Prize Banquet. When Dr. Martin Luther King Jr. won the Nobel Peace Prize in 1964, Mayor Ivan Allen Jr. asked Rabbi Rothschild, a personal friend of the King family, to chair a banquet honoring Atlanta's first Nobel laureate. A large percentage of the planning committee that Rabbi Rothschild assembled were members of the Jewish community. The testimonial dinner organized to honor Dr. King was attended by the local civic and clerical leaders in the community

and was the first integrated banquet in Atlanta history. Rothschild's wife, Janice, personally designed the engraved Steuben glass bowl presented to Dr. King. The bowl is now on display, alongside the Nobel Peace Prize, at the King Center. Pictured above is Rabbi Jacob Rothschild presenting the bowl to King at the banquet on January 27, 1965. (Courtesy of the Associated Press.)

The Goldstein Brothers. Born in Atlanta to Jewish immigrants fleeing persecution in Russia, Drs. Irving (left) and Marvin Goldstein (below) were early accomplished dentists and early outspoken civil rights advocates. Their dental practices were the first to treat Black patients from all over the Southeast. They also helped transform the Morris Hirsch Clinic into the Ben Massell Dental Clinic, which provides dental care to the less fortunate; the clinic still exists today. In 1948, they opened the Peachtree Manor Hotel, the first integrated hotel in Atlanta, and later built the Americana Motor Hotel, the first new hotel in downtown Atlanta in over 40 years. The Americana's policy in support of integration was a key factor in the relocation of the Milwaukee Braves to Atlanta. The hotel also served as a meeting place for civil rights leaders. Marvin Goldstein purchased the Georgian Terrace Hotel in 1961, saving it from destruction. The cast of *Gone with the Wind* stayed there for the film's Atlanta premiere in 1939. All three buildings still stand today. The Peachtree Manor Hotel and Georgian Terrace are listed in the National Register of Historic Places.

Dr. Ronald Goldstein. The son of Dr. Irving Goldstein and nephew of Dr. Marvin Goldstein, Dr. Ronald Goldstein followed in their footsteps and became a prominent dentist in his own right. A pioneer in the field of aesthetic dentistry, he also served as the first team dentist to the Atlanta Braves, the team his father and uncle helped bring to Atlanta by opening an integrated hotel downtown. Pictured is Hank Aaron (left) describing dental pain to Dr. Goldstein around 1974.

Elaine Barron Alexander. A native of Massachusetts, Alexander settled in Atlanta with her husband, Miles, in 1958. Recognizing the need for social change in the city, she became active in politics and women's issues. Alexander supported the political campaigns of Maynard Jackson, John Lewis, Elliott Levitas, Michael Dukakis, Shirley Franklin, and Kasim Reed. In addition, she served as vice chair of the Georgia Democratic Party and executive director of Leadership Atlanta from 1978 to 1992. Also active in the Jewish community, Alexander is a founding member of the Atlanta Black-Jewish Coalition and serves as a life board member of the American Jewish Committee and the Southeast Region's Anti-Defamation League.

Sherry Zimmerman Frank. A native Atlantan, Sherry Frank has worked in the Jewish community for more than 50 years. She served as the Southeast area director of the American Jewish Committee (AJC) from 1980 to 2006. Under her leadership, the AJC created the Atlanta Black-Jewish Coalition and the Atlanta Jewish Film Festival, now the largest Jewish film festival in the world.

Atlanta Black-Jewish Coalition. Spearheaded by the American Jewish Committee, the coalition was created in 1982 by members of Atlanta's Black and Jewish communities, which campaigned to renew the Voting Rights Act (VRA). Their efforts succeeded in renewing the VRA and reinvigorated the bond between the two communities. Today, the coalition continues to build on its original mission by providing a forum for meaningful dialogue and action. Pictured in 1985 are, from left to right, Sherry Frank, Cecil Alexander, Congressman John Lewis, and Elaine Alexander at the Edmund Pettus Bridge in Selma, Alabama, prior to the 20th anniversary of the civil rights march from Selma to Montgomery. (Courtesy of Sherry Frank.)

Six

Boomtown

In 1959, we were known for Coca-Cola, Georgia Tech, dogwoods, the Atlanta Crackers and easy Southern living; by 1969 we were known for gleaming skyscrapers, expressways, and the Atlanta Braves.

—Mayor Ivan Allen Jr.

By the late 1960s, much of the racial tension had quieted, and Atlanta experienced a massive boom that propelled the city into the national spotlight. In just a few decades, the sprawling skyline and infrastructure known today began to take shape. The Jewish community contributed to the rapid growth during this unique time in the city's history. It also helped set the stage for the quintessential international spotlight—hosting the 1996 Centennial Olympic Games.

Cementing Atlanta as a hub for professional sports, the Atlanta Falcons football franchise held its inaugural season in 1965. The following year, the Milwaukee Braves moved to the city and became the Atlanta Braves. To house these two new teams, the city built the Atlanta–Fulton County Stadium, designed by the notable homegrown architect Cecil Alexander, a Jewish community leader and civil rights activist. Alexander also designed several other iconic Atlanta landmarks, including The Coca-Cola Company headquarters, AT&T Midtown Center, and the Georgia Power corporate headquarters.

Embraced once again, members of the Jewish community reentered politics, largely for the first time since the 1915 lynching of Leo M. Frank. Sam Massell was elected Atlanta's first Jewish mayor; Elliott Levitas became Georgia's first Jewish US congressman; Stuart Eizenstat and Robert Lipshutz held prominent roles in presidential administrations; and Barbara Asher, Sidney Marcus, and Cathey Steinberg held local political offices.

Between 1970 and 1990, the Jewish community expanded from 16,500 to 65,000 throughout the metro area. Jewish life flourished as businesses, day schools, summer camps, and new congregations proliferated, catering to all aspects of Jewish life.

Alfred Davis. After gaining experience in the alcohol industry, Davis moved to Atlanta and cofounded National Distributing Company (NDC) in 1942. Under his leadership, NDC grew into the second-largest wine and spirit distributor in the country. Philanthropically, Davis supported countless charitable organizations and was named Philanthropist of the Year in 1991 by the Atlanta chapter of the Association of Fundraising Professionals. In 1992, his children created the Alfred and Adele Davis Academy, the first Reform Jewish day school in Atlanta. Pictured here is Davis (third from left) with NDC executives arriving in New York City around 1950.

Hebrew Academy of Atlanta. Established in 1953, the academy was the city's first Jewish day school. During the population boom following integration, numerous other Jewish day schools were established. In 2014, Hebrew Academy of Atlanta, then known as Greenfield Hebrew Academy, merged with Yeshiva High School to form Atlanta Jewish Academy. Pictured here is the first kindergarten class at Hebrew Academy of Atlanta in 1954.

The Jewish Home. By 1946, the Atlanta Federation for Jewish Social Services, presently the Jewish Federation of Greater Atlanta, and the newly formed Jewish Community Council began to address the needs of the elderly. A study of the metro Jewish population in 1947, funded by the Federation, highlighted the necessity for a facility based on the growing number and higher percentage of the aged in the total population. In 1950, Ben Massell donated a parcel of land on Fourteenth and Holly Streets to establish a residential facility for the elderly. The following year the home opened with a 30-bed capacity. During the next decade, the home doubled its capacity to 60 beds. By 1964, the booming population of Atlanta demanded even further expansions. Local businessman William Breman was appointed chairman of a long-range planning committee. Under his leadership, a new facility was constructed to meet the growing needs of the community. In 1967, property was purchased at Margaret Mitchell Drive and Howell Mill Road. On February 16, 1971, the new home opened. It was later renamed the William Breman Jewish Home and is now part of Jewish HomeLife, a nonprofit that addresses every stage of the aging journey. Pictured above are Jewish Home residents enjoying recreational therapy around 1970. Below is the Jewish Home around 1975.

Dr. Nanette Kass Wenger. Born in New York City to Jewish immigrants from Eastern Europe, Dr. Wenger settled in Atlanta in 1958 after becoming one of the first women to graduate from Harvard Medical School. She became the chief cardiologist at Grady Memorial Hospital and a professor of medicine at Emory University. Dr. Wenger conducted pioneering research on heart disease in women, initially believed to primarily affect men. She has received numerous awards for her work, including the Gold Heart Award, the highest honor given by the American Heart Association.

Esther Kahn Taylor. Born in Atlanta in 1905 to immigrants from Eastern Europe, Taylor was an accomplished musician, attending both Julliard in New York City and the Sorbonne in Paris. She was also a respected community activist. In 1964, Taylor brought together community leaders to create, fundraise, and establish the city's first Planned Parenthood affiliate—Planned Parenthood Association of the Atlanta Area Inc. The Esther and Herbert Taylor Oral History Collection at the William Breman Jewish Heritage Museum, consisting of more than a thousand interviews, is named for her and her husband.

ERWIN ZABAN. Born in Atlanta in 1921, Erwin Zaban became a prominent businessman and philanthropist. In 1937, his father, Mandle Zaban, founded Zep Manufacturing, a chemical company. Erwin started working for his father at age 15. In 1962, Zep merged with several other companies to form National Service Industries Inc., with Erwin Zaban as president. Erwin became increasingly involved in the Jewish community in the mid-1950s when he headed a fundraising campaign for the Atlanta Jewish Federation. His involvement included generous donations of his time and resources to establish Zaban Park, which became the home of the Atlanta Jewish Community Center, now the Marcus Jewish Community Center of Atlanta; the Temple Night Shelter for homeless couples, now the Zaban Paradies Center; and the Zaban Tower for affordable independent living on the Jewish HomeLife campus. Pictured below is National Service Industries executives around 1965; Erwin Zaban is seated second from right.

Atlanta Jewish Federation. In 1967, the Federation of Jewish Charities, the Atlanta Jewish Welfare Federation, and the Atlanta Jewish Community Council merged to form the Atlanta Jewish Federation, which operates today as the Jewish Federation of Greater Atlanta. Prior to the merger, each agency acted semi-independently in separate offices but with overlapping boards of directors. With a flourishing Jewish population, the merger consolidated social services under one organization to better serve the community. Pictured is the Federation building on Peachtree Street around 1970.

Betty Ann Romm Jacobson. A native Atlantan, Jacobson committed herself to a life of community service. She held leadership positions with the American Jewish Committee, the Temple, United Way, and Oakland Cemetery Historical Foundation. In 1986, Jacobson became the first female president of the Atlanta Jewish Federation, today the Jewish Federation of Greater Atlanta.

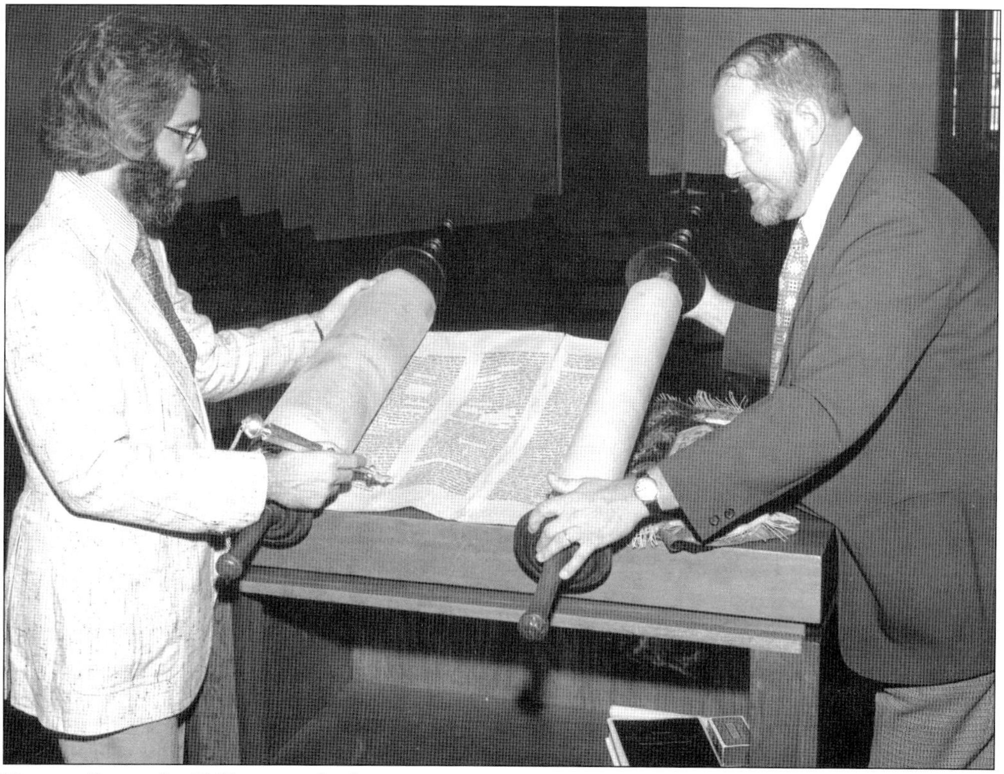

TEMPLE SINAI. In 1968, a new Reform Jewish congregation was organized for the first time since the Temple's founding in 1867. Located in the northern suburb of Sandy Springs, a newly emerging hub where many Jewish families had begun to settle, the congregation has grown to become one of the metro area's largest and most active congregations. Pictured is founding rabbi Richard Lehrman (left) reading from the Torah in 1975, with congregation president Gary Metzel.

JAN LINCOVE EPSTEIN. A Louisiana native, Epstein moved to Atlanta in 1956 to work for Delta Airlines. She quickly became involved in the Jewish community and was instrumental in the founding of Temple Sinai. She later became president of the congregation, the first woman president at any synagogue in Atlanta.

Sam Massell. In 1970, native Atlantan Samuel A. Massell Jr. became the first Jewish mayor of Atlanta, winning the election by securing 90 percent of the Black vote. During his tenure, he championed the building of the Omni Coliseum, an indoor arena. Billed as the "Madison Square Garden of the South," the Omni attracted eager fans to Atlanta Hawks basketball games and a myriad of featured entertainment in the multiuse space. Massell also established Woodruff Park, a green space in the heart of downtown Atlanta, and advocated for the creation of the Metro Atlanta Rapid Transit Authority, the main public transport system in the city. His vice mayor Maynard Jackson succeeded him in 1974, becoming the first Black mayor of Atlanta. Pictured below is Sam Massell signing a proclamation in support of Soviet Jewry in 1972.

RONALD M. BLOMBERG. A native Atlantan, Blomberg was drafted in 1967 by the New York Yankees. During his nearly decade-long career with the team, he became the first major leaguer to play a game as a designated hitter. A fan favorite, the famed Stage Deli in New York City even named a sandwich after him. Blomberg later played for the Chicago White Sox and managed the Bet Shemesh Blue Sox in the Israel Baseball League.

DR. DAVID R. BLUMENTHAL. In 1976, a Jewish studies program was inaugurated at Emory University with the creation of the Jay and Leslie Cohen Professorship, which was held by Dr. Blumenthal until his retirement in 2019. In 1999, the university broadened its commitment to this area of scholarship by establishing an interdisciplinary program focusing on all aspects of the Jewish experience, now known as the Rabbi Donald A. Tam Institute for Jewish Studies. As one of the region's leading centers for Jewish studies, the Tam Institute boasts more than a dozen core faculty members specializing in Jewish history, religion, literature, and culture. Emory is also home to a vibrant program devoted to the study of modern Israel, founded by Dr. Kenneth W. Stein.

Robert Lipshutz. A native Atlantan, Lipshutz was national campaign treasurer for Jimmy Carter's successful 1976 presidential bid and was appointed White House counsel in the Carter administration. He played a significant role in brokering the negotiations between Israel and Egypt that led to the historic signing of the Camp David Accords in 1978. Lipshutz later served as a trustee for the Atlanta Jewish Federation and the Carter Center.

President's Commission on the Holocaust. Charged by President Carter to create a report outlining the most appropriate way to establish and maintain a memorial to those who perished in the Holocaust, the commission's advice led to the founding of the US Holocaust Memorial Museum in Washington, DC. Jewish Atlantans played prominent roles on the commission. Pictured in 1979 is Speaker of the House Tip O'Neill (far right) swearing in former president of the Atlanta section of the National Council of Jewish Women Marilyn Shubin (far left); Holocaust survivor Cantor Isaac Goodfriend (second from left); activist and Holocaust history expert Sylvia Becker (center); and Robert Lipshutz (third from right). The chair of the commission, Elie Wiesel, is holding the Bible.

STUART EIZENSTAT. Born in Chicago and raised in Atlanta, Eizenstat is an accomplished, respected attorney and policymaker. He served many prominent roles in several presidential administrations, including ambassador to the European Union. He is also recognized for his extensive work on Holocaust restitution, as well as founding the Fran Eizenstat & Eizenstat Family Memorial Lecture Series at Ahavath Achim Synagogue. Since 1988, this free, public event has featured well-known speakers such as Ruth Bader Ginsburg and Madeleine Albright addressing current and thought-provoking issues.

CAMP BARNEY MEDINTZ. Founded in 1963 in Cleveland, Georgia, Camp Barney Medintz was the first permanent overnight summer camp for the Atlanta Jewish Community Center. It was named in honor of Barney Medintz, who was deeply beloved and heavily involved in Jewish youth activities before passing away at age 50. Today, Camp Barney, in addition to the other two Jewish summer camps in Georgia, Camp Coleman and Ramah Darom, serves thousands of boys and girls from throughout the Southeast each summer. Pictured are campers playing tug-of-war at Camp Barney Medintz around 1975.

ELLIOTT LEVITAS. A native Atlantan, Elliott H. Levitas served in the Georgia House of Representatives and in the US House of Representatives. He represented Georgia's 4th Congressional District, a major section of metro Atlanta. In 1996, Levitas helped bring the largest class-action lawsuit in history against the federal government on behalf of Elouise Cobell and other Native Americans. The case was eventually settled in 2009 for $3.4 billion and provided justice to hundreds of thousands of Native Americans whose trust funds had been mismanaged by the US government. Pictured below is Congressman Levitas (far left) with Pres. Jimmy Carter in the Cabinet Room of the White House in 1977.

The Home Depot. Newly arrived in Atlanta, entrepreneurs Bernie Marcus and Arthur Blank (above) founded The Home Depot in 1978. What began with two stores in the Atlanta metro area grew into an international company and household name by the end of the century. Along the way, Marcus and Blank have given back to the city that gave them their start. Bernie Marcus established the Marcus Autism Center, the Marcus Jewish Community Center of Atlanta, the Marcus Hillel Center at Emory University, the Marcus Trauma and Marcus Stroke and Neuroscience Centers at Grady Hospital, and the Georgia Aquarium. Arthur Blank owns two professional sports teams—the Atlanta Falcons and Atlanta United FC—both play in the Mercedes-Benz Stadium, which he helped build. Their individual philanthropic foundations, the Arthur Blank Family Foundation and the Billi and Bernie Marcus Foundation, combined, have donated close to a billion dollars to important causes over the years. Pictured at right is Bernie Marcus (left) at the ribbon cutting of an early Home Depot store in 1979.

Barbara Miller Asher. A Wisconsin native, Asher moved to Atlanta in 1963 and became an active community volunteer. In 1974, Mayor Maynard Jackson appointed her to the city's zoning review board. In 1977, Asher was elected to the Atlanta City Council and served for three terms. During her tenure as a city councilwoman, she facilitated the zoning and restoration of the Fairlie-Poplar historic district of downtown Atlanta. A statue was erected in her memory on the green space of Marietta Street adjacent to the historic district she helped preserve. Pictured above is Barbara Asher (left) campaigning for Atlanta City Council alongside fellow politician Cathey Steinberg in 1977. At left is Asher's family at the dedication of the statue erected in her memory in downtown Atlanta on May 29, 1998.

Cathey Weiss Steinberg. A Pennsylvania native, Cathey Steinberg moved to Atlanta in 1971. She served in the Georgia General Assembly for 16 years in both the Georgia House of Representatives (1977–1989) and in the Georgia Senate (1991–1993). Steinberg is recognized as a strong advocate for women's rights and was the primary sponsor of the 1981–1982 Equal Rights Amendment legislation.

Sidney J. Marcus. Atlanta native Sidney Marcus served 14 years in the Georgia House of Representatives. He displayed the ability to work across the aisle to pass major legislation and led efforts to fight plans by the state to build a highway from downtown to Stone Mountain, successfully preserving several historic in-town neighborhoods. In 1981, Marcus ran for mayor but lost the election to civil rights leader and former US ambassador to the United Nations Andrew Young. Sidney Marcus Boulevard, a major thoroughfare in the city, is named in his memory. Marcus is pictured here campaigning for mayor in 1981.

Driving Miss Daisy. The 1987 play *Driving Miss Daisy*, later adapted to film, chronicled the complex relationship between an elderly Jewish woman and her Black chauffeur during the period of segregation. It won numerous awards including a Pulitzer Prize for Drama, several Academy Awards, and Golden Globes. Its author, Alfred Uhry, born and raised in Atlanta, based the character of Miss Daisy on his grandmother Lena Guthman Fox and her friends. Pictured is Lena Guthman Fox (standing) with her friends in 1947.

YOEL LEVI. Born in Romania and reared in Israel, Yoel Levi came to Atlanta in 1988 to be the music director at the Atlanta Symphony Orchestra. Under his leadership, the ASO recorded numerous albums with the esteemed record label Telarc and was nominated Best Orchestra of the Year in the 1991–1992 International Classical Music Awards. Levi served as director of the ASO until 2000 and director emeritus until 2005.

Soviet Jewry. During the second half of the 20th century, Atlanta's Jews grew increasingly concerned with international struggles confronting the Jewish people. The burgeoning State of Israel came under frequent attacks by its Arab neighbors, and Jews living in the Soviet Union could not openly practice their religion or leave the country. The Atlanta Jewish community stood in solidarity with Jews trapped behind the Iron Curtain. Rallies were held to aid refugee services, sign petitions, and lobby politicians to support the cause. At right are Jewish Soviet refugees arriving in Atlanta on March 9, 1979. The c. 1988 photograph below is of a rally in Atlanta to support Soviet Jewry.

Congregation Bet Haverim. During the early days of the AIDS epidemic, members of the Jewish community who identified as LGBTQ did not feel accepted by the established synagogues in Atlanta. Spearheaded by Gary Piccola, Congregation Bet Haverim was established in 1985. The synagogue has grown into a vibrant and diverse congregation, which affiliates with the Reconstructionist movement. Pictured in 1988 are Sherry Emory (left), president of Congregation Bet Haverim, and Ruth Anne Davis preparing the ark that the congregation used to celebrate the High Holidays. (Photograph by Dwight Ross Jr., courtesy of the Associated Press.)

Cecil Alexander. Native Atlantan Cecil A. Alexander Jr. was a World War II dive bomber pilot, a renowned architect, and an outspoken activist during the civil rights movement. He influenced Atlanta's physical appearance as well as its political, social, and racial structure. Alexander designed several iconic buildings in Atlanta and served on the building committees for the Martin Luther King Center and Clark Atlanta University. Pictured is Alexander (right) meeting with Pres. George H.W. Bush and Vice Pres. Dan Quayle around 1990.

Seven

THE OLYMPIC GAMES

We have in our minds the tragedy of Munich where eleven Israeli athletes were killed during the Olympic Games in 1972. . . . More than ever we have fully committed to building a better more peaceful world in which forms of terrorism are eradicated and now please join me in a moment of silence to honor all victims.

—Juan Antonio Samaranch
President, International Olympic Committee, August 4, 1996

In just a century and a half, a small railroad junction grew into a vibrant city that audaciously catapulted itself onto the international stage by hosting the summer 1996 Centennial Olympic Games. Atlantans embraced the magnitude of the moment. As the city busily prepared to entertain the world, so too did Atlanta's Jewish community.

Prior to Atlanta hosting the Olympics, two philanthropic businessmen—William Breman and Steve Selig—generously donated funds and land, respectively, to construct a facility to house the offices of the Atlanta Jewish Federation, presently the Jewish Federation of Greater Atlanta, and a museum to showcase Atlanta's rich Jewish history. Located in Midtown Atlanta, the Selig Center opened shortly before the start of the Olympics. The William Breman Jewish Heritage Museum, comprised of three galleries and an archival repository, continues to serve the Atlanta community and connect people to Jewish history, culture, and arts.

The Federation viewed the Olympic Games as an opportunity to honor the memory of the Israeli athletes slain by terrorists during the 1972 Munich games. The International Olympic Committee (IOC) had never officially recognized the tragedy. The Federation's memorialization efforts culminated during the closing ceremony of the games when Juan Samaranch, president of the IOC, held a moment of silence in memory of the murdered Israeli athletes and those who were affected by the bombing in Centennial Olympic Park, which occurred on the eighth day of the Atlanta Games.

Influencing a recalcitrant, powerful international body to acknowledge a tragic event in Jewish history was a significant moment for Jews in Atlanta and around the world. This recognition highlighted the strength of the people and organizations that make up the Atlanta Jewish community.

M. William Breman. As a child, Breman moved to Atlanta from North Carolina in 1913 when his father accepted the position of office manager at Stein Junk Company. He eventually took over the business and renamed it Breman Steel Company, expanding the business to include steel fabrication. Throughout his lifetime, Breman held leadership positions in many organizations and received several distinguished awards that reflected his support for the Jewish community. The William Breman Jewish Home and the William Breman Jewish Heritage Museum are both named in his honor. Through her own involvement in and commitment to the Jewish community, Breman's daughter Carol Nemo continues her father's charitable legacy through the Breman Family Foundation.

Elinor Angel Rosenberg Breman. Born in Chattanooga in 1922, Elinor moved to Atlanta after marrying her first husband, Herbert Rosenberg Jr., whom she met at Ballyhoo. Throughout her storied life, which included running an art gallery and a successful career in real estate, Elinor was actively involved in the Jewish community. In 1993, she married widower William Breman and, with him, was a driving force behind the creation of the William Breman Jewish Heritage Museum. The couple is pictured here cutting the ribbon at the opening ceremony of the Breman in 1996.

DAVID SARNAT. As executive director of the Atlanta Jewish Federation from 1979 to 2000, Sarnat was instrumental in implementing many significant projects and lobbying efforts for the growing community. When William Breman approached the Federation with a major gift, David Sarnat suggested the donation be allocated toward a museum dedicated to the history of Jewish Atlanta.

JANE DENABURG LEAVEY. In 1983, Atlanta Jewish Federation employee Jane Leavey curated the exhibition "Jews and Georgians: A Meeting of Cultures, 1733–1983," which was displayed in Emory University's Schatten Gallery. The success of the exhibit inspired a movement to establish a permanent museum that preserves and interprets Jewish history in Georgia. Leavey became the lead contact at the Federation, helping to establish both the Jewish Community Archives, now the Ida Pearle and Joseph Cuba Archives for Southern Jewish History, and the William Breman Jewish Heritage Museum. She served as founding executive director of the Breman from 1996 to 2011. Pictured here is Leavey leading a tour at the opening of the Breman in 1996.

Sandra Katz Berman. Born and raised in Cleveland, Ohio, Berman was the founding archivist of the Cleveland Jewish Archives at the Western Reserve Historical Society. She later moved to Atlanta, and in 1985 became the founding archivist of the Ida Pearle and Joseph Cuba Archives for Southern Jewish History at the William Breman Jewish Heritage Museum. During her 28-year tenure, Berman cocurated multiple exhibitions at the Breman and expanded the scope of the museum to include collections from Jewish communities throughout Georgia and surrounding states.

Joseph and Ida Pearle Miller Cuba. In 1995, the Cuba family donated the funds to transform the Jewish Community Archives into a state-of-the-art facility at the William Breman Jewish Heritage Museum. The Ida Pearle and Joseph Cuba Archives for Southern Jewish History is now the largest repository in the Southeast for Southern Jewish history. The images for this book draw largely from the extensive photography collections housed in the archives.

The Selig Center. With a lineage of community leaders in Atlanta, the Selig family generously donated the property to create the Selig Center, which houses the Jewish Federation of Greater Atlanta and the William Breman Jewish Heritage Museum. In 1994, Steve Selig helped start another cultural icon in the city—Music Midtown, an annual music festival that takes place in Piedmont Park. Pictured around 1995 is Steve Selig with his sister Cathy Kuranoff (left) and his wife, Linda, as they inspect the Selig Center construction plans.

Helen Wasserman Spiegel. Born in Nuremberg, Germany, Helen and her family escaped Nazi Germany in 1938 and settled in the United States. She moved to Atlanta in 1946 after marrying fellow Holocaust survivor Frank Spiegel. Helen's volunteer activities in the Jewish community were wide-ranging. She was an early supporter of the Atlanta Hebrew Academy, a regional president of Hadassah, and along with Frank, organized and ran the Shearith Israel Synagogue women's night shelter. As a Holocaust survivor, she readily shared her story with school groups and organizations all over Atlanta. In 1996, she was honored for her volunteer efforts in the community and nominated as an Olympic torch runner.

Memorial Dedication Ceremony. To honor the memory of the 11 Israeli athletes murdered at the 1972 Munich Olympics, the Atlanta Jewish Federation invited family members of the athletes to participate in the dedication of a memorial on the grounds of the newly inaugurated Selig Center. Thanks to the lobbying efforts of the Federation, the athletes' descendants belatedly received recognition from the International Olympic Committee during the Games' closing ceremony. Pictured are descendants of the slain Israeli Olympic athletes gathering around the memorial on July 19, 1996.

Dr. Deborah E. Lipstadt. Just one month after the Centennial Olympic Games' closing ceremony, the city was once again thrust into the international spotlight. On September 5, 1996, David Irving sued Emory University professor Deborah Lipstadt and her publisher Penguin Books in an English court for labeling him a Holocaust denier in her book *Denying the Holocaust: The Growing Assault on Truth and Memory*. She won the case. Dr. Lipstadt's book *Denial*, which documents her courtroom experience, later became a 2016 historical drama film starring British actress Rachel Weisz as Dr. Lipstadt.

Eight

The Next Century

Supported by the efforts of numerous Jewish institutions in the city that are reaching out across lines of geography, background, and denomination to create an ongoing feeling of unity amid diversity . . . there is every reason to believe that the Atlanta Jewish community will continue to thrive well beyond its next century.

—Dr. Eric Goldstein,
A History of Jews in Atlanta: To Life, 2006

Similar to the boom Atlanta experienced following the Civil War and again after the civil rights movement, hosting the Olympics spurred economic growth that thrust the city into the 21st century. Atlanta has continued its role as a major transportation hub. Since 2000, Hartsfield-Jackson International Airport has held the title of world's busiest airport. Akin to the railroads that spawned the city, the airport has provided a steady stream of raw goods, materials, and entrepreneurial trailblazers that continue to fuel the city's growth.

In 2006, the Jewish Federation of Greater Atlanta conducted a population survey, which found that 81 percent of Jews in the city were not native Atlantans. This statistic highlighted the arrival of new settlers to the city from around the globe seeking the American dream. The report also concluded that Atlanta's Jewish population had topped 100,000, making the community one of the largest in the country.

With the influx of newcomers to the Jewish community, Atlanta has become an innovation incubator. This century has already witnessed the emergence of countless creative local Jewish organizations and businesses that span arts, culture, entertainment, and medicine—several of which have developed global recognition. A diverse range of annual events has developed that showcase Jewish film, life, literature, and music. Featuring world-renowned headliners, the Atlanta Jewish Book Festival, Film Festival, Life Festival, and Music Festival attract tens of thousands of attendees. Atlanta also continues to be a beacon for the expansion of contemporary national and international organizations such as Birthright Israel, Honeymoon Israel, Limmud, Moishe House, OneTable, PJ Library, and Repair the World—all of which have opened local or regional hubs in the city.

As Atlanta and its Jewish community continue to write yet another chapter in the city's storied 175-year history, the future, informed by the past, presents limitless opportunities for Jewish contribution to the city and beyond.

Buckhead Coalition. In 1989, former mayor of Atlanta Sam Massell founded the Buckhead Coalition. The organization, comprised of business and civic leaders, is dedicated to establishing and implementing action programs for the continued improvement of businesses and residential areas in Atlanta's Buckhead neighborhood. For more than 30 years, Massell served as president and is affectionately known as the unofficial "mayor of Buckhead." Due to his leadership, Buckhead now boasts its own skyline and is Atlanta's most successful commercial and residential area. Pictured is Massell overlooking Buckhead with the Atlanta skyline in the distance. (Courtesy of Daemon Baizan/DAEMONpictures.)

Operation Isaiah. For the past three decades, the Jewish community, spearheaded by Ahavath Achim Synagogue, has partnered with the Atlanta Community Food Bank to help alleviate the lack of adequate food for thousands of fellow citizens. The annual campaign, known as Operation Isaiah, is held during the High Holiday season and is now the largest religious-based food drive in Atlanta. Encouraging further involvement, the food bank moved its annual Hunger Walk from Saturday to Sunday to allow greater participation from the Jewish community. Pictured here is Mayor Maynard Jackson participating in the first Operation Isaiah in 1991. (Courtesy of Doris Goldstein.)

SUPPORT FOR ISRAEL. Atlanta's Jewish community has continued its unabated support for the State of Israel into the 21st century. Working through various partnership programs, the Jewish Federation of Greater Atlanta formed a sister city relationship with the Israeli communities of Yokneam and Megiddo. The association has led to a range of educational, cultural, and religious exchange programs. Pictured here is Steve Selig, Federation president, riding a camel through Midtown Atlanta during the 50th anniversary celebration of Israel's independence in 1998. (Photograph by Dwight Ross Jr., courtesy of the Associated Press.)

MARCUS JEWISH COMMUNITY CENTER AT ZABAN PARK. In April 2000, the Atlanta Jewish Community Center was renamed the Marcus Jewish Community Center of Atlanta (MJCCA) and expanded with a new main building. Featuring indoor and outdoor sports facilities, meeting rooms, and multipurpose spaces, the MJCCA annually impacts more than 60,000 people of all backgrounds. Pictured is the entrance to the Zaban-Blank Building around 2000. (Courtesy of the MJCCA.)

Atlanta Jewish Film Festival (AJFF). Founded in 2000 by the Atlanta Regional Office of the American Jewish Committee, the AJFF fosters stronger bonds within the Jewish community and intergroup relations with Atlanta's diverse cultural, ethnic, and religious communities through the shared experience of cinematic storytelling. Under the leadership of Kenny Blank, the annual event has quickly grown into the largest Jewish film festival in the world. Pictured is closing night in 2019. (Courtesy of AJFF.)

Jennings Hertz Jr. Giving up his acting ambitions to run the family business, Jennings Hertz Jr. grew United Distributors into the largest alcoholic beverage wholesaler in both Georgia and Alabama. A major supporter of the arts in Atlanta, the Alliance Theatre renamed its intimate, 200-seat stage in his honor. Following his wife's death in 2001, he endowed in perpetuity the Jill Hertz Principal Flute Chair at the Atlanta Symphony Orchestra. Hertz's son Doug followed in his footsteps both with operating the family business and philanthropic endeavors, and founding Camp Twin Lakes, a year-round, fully accessible, specially designed camp for children with disabilities.

Compromise Flag. In 1956, Georgia adopted a new state flag incorporating the Confederate battle emblem. In the late 20th century, opposition to the flag steadily grew. Renowned architect and social activist Cecil Alexander proposed a new design, which was approved by the Georgia legislature in 2001. This "compromise flag" (pictured) served until 2004, when it was replaced by the current flag.

Pride. In 2001, Southern Jewish Resource Network for Gender and Sexual Diversity (SOJOURN), formerly the Rainbow Center, was founded by Atlanta native and spiritual leader of Congregation Bet Haverim Rabbi Joshua Lesser. Advancing gender and sexual diversity support and empowerment by building inclusive communities through Jewish values, the faith-based agency offers a variety of training workshops, outreach programs, and advocacy initiatives. SOJOURN also coordinates the Jewish community's involvement in the annual Atlanta Pride Parade. (Courtesy of SOJOURN.)

Georgia Aquarium. After visiting dozens of aquariums around the world, Home Depot cofounder Bernie Marcus and his wife, Billi, decided to donate funds to build one in Atlanta. When the Georgia Aquarium opened in 2005, it was the largest in the world. Consisting of seven major galleries with more than 10 million gallons of fresh and saltwater, the aquarium researches and houses hundreds of species and thousands of marine animals. (Courtesy of the Georgia Aquarium.)

Eva Cohn Galambos. Escaping fascist Europe, Eva Galambos settled in Georgia, where she earned business and economics degrees from the University of Georgia and Georgia State University respectively. Years later, Galambos spearheaded a three-decade effort to create Georgia's first new city since World War II. When Sandy Springs was incorporated in 2005, she was elected its first mayor and served until 2013. She is pictured at her swearing-in ceremony with her husband, John, on December 1, 2005. (Courtesy of the City of Sandy Springs.)

JScreen. In 2009, Atlantans Randy and Caroline Gold learned that their daughter Eden had been born with a terminal genetic disease. Turning adversity into action, the Golds founded JScreen, a national nonprofit public health initiative that provides affordable, at-home, saliva-based carrier screening and genetic counseling. With support from the Marcus Foundation and Emory University School of Medicine, the program has enabled innumerable prospective parents to determine their risk of passing on inherited conditions that are more common in the Jewish community. (Courtesy of the Gold family.)

Emory Apology. In 2012, Emory University formally apologized for the deep-rooted antisemitism within its dental school from 1948 to 1961. During his tenure, the dean of the dental school, John Buhler, failed 65 percent of the Jewish students in the program. Years later, one of the students, Dr. Perry Brickman (pictured), began investigating the high numbers of Jewish expulsions that occurred under Dean Buhler. He helped bring the situation to light after creating a detailed documentary exposing the scandal. Honoring his extensive research, Emory University awarded Dr. Brickman the Emory Maker of History Award and the Emory Medal. In 2019, he published the book *Extracted: Unmasking Rampant Antisemitism in America's Higher Education.* (Courtesy of Emory University Photo Video.)

Jewish Kids Groups (JKG). Founded in 2012 by Atlanta native Ana Fuchs Robbins, JKG is one of only a few independent Hebrew schools in the country. With a variety of programs for all types of Jewish families, including interfaith to unaffiliated, JKG has developed a diverse audience and redefined what Jewish education can be for underserved communities searching for Jewish identity. (Courtesy of JKG.)

Atlanta Kosher BBQ. Founded in 2013, the Atlanta Kosher BBQ Festival is a juried barbecue competition that maintains Jewish dietary laws. Open to the public, the competition offers samples of brisket, ribs, chicken, and chili, as well as live music and children's activities. In 2019, the festival attracted more than 4,000 visitors. Pictured are Dale and Michael Yoss of the BBQ'n Hebrew Hillbillies serving food samples to hungry customers on October 22, 2017. (Courtesy of John Awtrey.)

Chef Todd Ginsberg. Bringing his gastronomic talents to Atlanta after graduating from the Culinary Institute of America, Chef Todd Ginsberg has pioneered several popular restaurants in Atlanta. The General Muir, named after the ship that brought co-owner Jennifer Johnson's mother and grandparents to the United States after surviving the Holocaust, is a modern American restaurant inspired by classic New York Jewish delis. Chef Ginsberg also owns Yalla, a Middle Eastern food stand at Krog Street Market. Pictured in 2019 is Chef Ginsberg presenting a live cooking demonstration at Limmud Atlanta & Southeast. (Courtesy of Ori Salzberg.)

Congregation Ohr HaTorah. Founded in 1994 as Young Israel of Toco Hills, Congregation Ohr HaTorah aims to make Orthodox Judaism more relevant to a new generation of Jewish Atlantans. Under the guidance of executive director Eliana Leader, the congregation constructed the first Orthodox synagogue in the world built to environmental standards, achieving EarthCraft Light Commercial Gold-level certification in 2014. Their previous synagogue was sold to Congregation Bet Haverim and is still used today.

Mercedes-Benz Stadium. In 2017, Home Depot cofounder Arthur Blank opened a new multipurpose stadium in downtown Atlanta. The Mercedes-Benz Stadium is home to two professional sports teams, the Atlanta Falcons and Atlanta United FC, both owned by Blank. The stadium also hosts concerts and various other sporting events, including Super Bowl LIII in 2019. One of the many pieces of artwork displayed inside the stadium is a large sculpture featuring a Mishnaic quote from Hillel the Elder. (Courtesy of Wikimedia Commons.)

Oakland Cemetery. In 2016, the Rich Foundation granted Oakland Cemetery Foundation much of the funds needed to restore the cemetery's three Jewish burial sections. The project repaired tombstones and walkways and improved green spaces. While the Jewish community of Atlanta is now one of the largest and most vibrant in the country, it still proudly honors its past and humble origins.

About the William Breman Jewish Heritage Museum

The William Breman Jewish Heritage Museum is a preeminent center for Jewish culture in the Southeast, bringing people of all backgrounds together in understanding and appreciation of Jewish history, culture, and the arts. The Breman, located in Midtown Atlanta, houses, as part of the Lillian and A.J. Weinberg Center for Holocaust education, a permanent Holocaust exhibit as well as gallery and auditorium spaces hosting a range of other exhibits and performances.

The Breman began as a repository for local history; it was founded in 1985 as the Jewish Community Archives, now known as the Ida Pearle and Joseph Cuba Archives for Southern Jewish History. This archive is now the largest repository of Jewish history in the Southeast. The archives document Jewish life in the region since the colonial era and the lives of the many Holocaust survivors who settled here. Most of the images featured in this book are from the photography collections housed in the archives.

The Breman was named one of the Ten Best Museums in Atlanta by *USA Today*, Institution of the Year by the Georgia Association of Museums and Galleries, and a Must See Destination in Atlanta by TripAdvisor.com.

For more information, and to explore the museum and archive virtually, please visit www.thebreman.org.

Consistent with our mission to preserve history on a local level, this book was printed in South Carolina on American-made paper and manufactured entirely in the United States. Products carrying the accredited Forest Stewardship Council (FSC) label are printed on 100 percent FSC-certified paper.